First World War
and Army of Occupation
War Diary
France, Belgium and Germany

33 DIVISION
19 Infantry Brigade
Cameronians (Scottish Rifles)
5/6th Battalion
1 October 1918 - 31 October 1919

WO95/2422/5

The Naval & Military Press Ltd
www.nmarchive.com
Published in association with The National Archives

Published by

The Naval & Military Press Ltd

Unit 10 Ridgewood Industrial Park,

Uckfield, East Sussex,

TN22 5QE England

Tel: +44 (0) 1825 749494

www.naval-military-press.com

www.nmarchive.com

This diary has been reprinted in facsimile from the original. Any imperfections are inevitably reproduced and the quality may fall short of modern type and cartographic standards.

© Crown Copyright
Images reproduced by permission of The National Archives, London, England, 2015.

Contents

Document type	Place/Title	Date From	Date To
Heading	WO95/2422-5 5/6 Cameronians 1918 Oct. 1919 Oct		
Heading	33 Division 19 Bde 5/6 Scottish Rifles (Cameronians) 1918 Oct-1919 Oct		
War Diary	S.E. of Villers Guislain.	01/10/1918	31/10/1918
Miscellaneous	5/6th Scottish Rifles October, 1918 Casualties For Month		
Miscellaneous	5/6th Scottish Rifles. War Diary October, 1918 Appendix No. 1		
Miscellaneous	Commune de Clary. To G.O.C., 33rd Division.	11/10/1918	11/10/1918
Miscellaneous	5/6th Scottish Rifles. War Diary. October, 1918. Appendix No. 2		
Miscellaneous	C Form. Messages And Signals.		
Miscellaneous	5/6th Scottish Rifles. War Diary. October, 1918. Appendix No. 3		
Miscellaneous	Telegram To A.D.C. for G.O.C., 33rd Division.	26/10/1918	26/10/1918
Miscellaneous	5th/6th Scottish Rifles. War Diary. October, 1918. Appendix No. 4		
Miscellaneous	Copy Speech delivered by General, Shute, C.B., C.M.G. Commander-In-Chief V Corps on the occasion of his inspection of the 19th Infantry Brigade 29/10/18	29/10/1918	29/10/1918
Miscellaneous	5th/6th Scottish Rifles. War Diary. October, 1918. Appendix No. 5.		
Miscellaneous	5th/6th Scottish Rifles. Honors and Awards.		
War Diary	Troisvilles	01/11/1918	03/11/1918
War Diary	Englefontaine	04/11/1918	04/11/1918
War Diary	Mormal Forest	05/11/1918	05/11/1918
War Diary	Aulnoye.	06/11/1918	06/11/1918
War Diary	Ecuelin	07/11/1918	07/11/1918
War Diary	Sarbaras	08/11/1918	14/11/1918
War Diary	Locquignol	15/11/1918	15/11/1918
War Diary	Locquignol to Croix	16/11/1918	16/11/1918
War Diary	Clary	17/11/1918	30/11/1918
Miscellaneous	5th Battalion Scottish Rifles War Diary November 1918 Appendix No.1		
Miscellaneous	5th Scottish Rifles November 1918 Appendix No 1		
Heading	5th Battalion Scottish Rifles War Diary November 1918. Appendix No. 2		
Miscellaneous	5th Scottish Rifles November 1918 Appendix No. 2		
Heading	5th Battalion Scottish Rifles War Diary. November, 1918 Appendix No. 3		
Miscellaneous	Honours And Awards		
Heading	5th Battalion Scottish Rifles War Diary November, 1918. Appendix No 4.		
Heading	5th Battalion Scottish Rifles War Diary November 1918. Appendix No. 6		
Miscellaneous	A Form Messages And Signals.		
Heading	5th Battalion Scottish Rifles War Diary. November, 1918. Appendix No 5		
Miscellaneous	5th Scottish Rifles November 1918 Appendix No. 5		
War Diary	5th/6th Scottish Rifles December 1918	01/12/1918	31/12/1918

War Diary	Montagne	01/01/1919	31/01/1919
Heading	5/6th Bn. Scottish Rifles Appendix I War Diary January 1919		
Miscellaneous	City Chambers Glasgow. War Diary	11/01/1919	11/01/1919
Miscellaneous	Well Hall. Hamilton.	13/01/1919	13/01/1919
War Diary	Rouen	01/02/1919	28/02/1919
War Diary	Rouen.	01/03/1919	31/03/1919
Miscellaneous	5/6th Scottish Rifles. March 1919 Reinforcement Received During Month		
War Diary	Rouen	01/04/1919	30/04/1919
War Diary	Rouen.	01/05/1919	31/05/1919
War Diary	Rouen	01/06/1919	15/06/1919
War Diary	Calais	16/06/1919	30/06/1919
War Diary	Calais	01/07/1919	31/07/1919
War Diary	Calais	01/08/1919	31/08/1919
War Diary	Calais	01/09/1919	30/09/1919
War Diary	Beaumarais Calais	01/10/1919	31/10/1919

WO 95 2422/5

5/6 Cameronians
1915 Oct - 1919 Oct

33 DIVISION

19 COE

5/6 SCOTTISH RIFLES (CAMERONIANS)

1916 OCT — 1919 OCT

According to Order of Battle the
1/5 and 1/6 Bns amalgamated
in May 1916
Diaries have been rendered
separately

Army Form C. 2118.

WAR DIARY
or
INTELLIGENCE SUMMARY.
(Erase heading not required.)

Instructions regarding War Diaries and Intelligence Summaries are contained in F. S. Regs., Part II. and the Staff Manual respectively. Title pages will be prepared in manuscript.

Place	Date	Hour	Summary of Events and Information	Remarks and references to Appendices
			5/6th SCOTTISH RIFLES. OCTOBER, 1918.	H.Q.C. Wheler
S.E. of VILLERS GUISLAIN.	1		Situation unaltered.	
	2		Arrangements made to take over front of 1st MIDDLESEX Regt. and 2nd ARGYLL & SUTHERLAND HIGHLANDERS with four Companies of the Battalion in Sector E. and W. of HONNECOURT WOOD. This was successfully completed by 22.40 hours.	
	3/4		Forward posts were established commanding CANAL crossings. Enemy machine gun fire opposed all attempts by patrols to reach Eastern bank of CANAL.	
	5		About 7 a.m. our patrols crossed the CANAL at HONNECOURT and the village and ground in front was found clear of the enemy. With the 1st CAMERONIANS on the right the Battalion proceeded to take up a line N. and S. of Eastern edge of PRANQUE WOOD and patrols went on to LA TERRIERE without opposition. At 12.15 hours Companies in Artillery formation advanced on the following objectives:- LEFT A Coy. (1) BANCOURT FARM. (2) BONABUS FARM. LEFT CENTRE D " HINDENBURG LINE. (support.) RIGHT CENTRE C " (1) HINDENBURG LINE (Support)(2)LA TERRIERE WOOD. RIGHT B " LA TERRIERE. (Southern half.) and HINDENBURG SUPPORT LINE. These positions were secured with very slight machine gun opposition. Battalion Headquarters were established in LA TERRIERE.	
	6		Section posts consolidated. Companies remained in the new line and put out outposts during the night.	
	7		Troops of 38th Division went forward on the Right Divisional Sector in the morning to the line BOIS DE BOURLON (exclusive) - AUBENCHEUL - AUX BOIS (inclusive) and the Battalion remained in the line as Supports.	

Army Form C. 2118.

WAR DIARY
or
INTELLIGENCE SUMMARY.
(Erase heading not required.)

Instructions regarding War Diaries and Intelligence Summaries are contained in F. S. Regs., Part II. and the Staff Manual respectively. Title pages will be prepared in manuscript.

Place	Date	Hour	Summary of Events and Information	Remarks and references to Appendices
5/6TH SCOTTISH RIFLES.			OCTOBER, 1918.	
	8		The advance was continued by the 38th Division in the morning with the assistance of Tanks. Units on the flanks conformed. BOIS DE MORTHO and VILLERS OUTREAUX were cleared and after stiff fighting by dusk the Outpost line was east of MALINCOURT, the enemy still holding DEHERIES. At 16 hours the Battalion occupied the LE CATELET - MAUROY LINE.	
	9		After midnight (8/9th) 13th Brigade moved via AUBENCHEUL - AUX - BOIS and VILLERS OUTREAUX to MALINCOURT. 1st Queens on right and 5/6th Scottish Rifles on left deployed on line of 114th Brigade (38th Division) and at 05.20 hours passed through advancing N.E. on CLARY, B Company on Left, C Company Centre, A Company on right and D Company in Reserve. The enemy had withdrawn and no resistance was met till Companies appeared on eastern outskirts of CLARY. This was eventually overcome, Cavalry assisting, and our outposts dug in on Crest E. of village. Battalion Headquarters in CLARY. Captured :- 5 Officers, 50 Other Ranks. (Lord STRATHCONA'S HORSE.) 41 Other Ranks. Field Guns. 3 Machine Guns. not counted. Horses. 5	No.1.
	10	07.00 hours	Battalion moved to Billets in BERTRY and came into Div. Reserve.	
	11		Battalion at BERTRY resting and cleaning up. Letter of thanks received by Division from the Maire of CLARY - vide appendix No.1. Brigade moved to MALINCOURT Area - Battalion accommodated in Billets.	
	12			
	13		Battalion inspected on parade and addressed by Divisional Commander.	
	14		During the forenoon Companies were engaged in training in open ground outside MALINCOURT. In the evening a Battalion concert was held in the	

Army Form C. 2118.

WAR DIARY
or
INTELLIGENCE SUMMARY.
(Erase heading not required.)

Place	Date	Hour	Summary of Events and Information	Remarks and references to Appendices
5/6TH SCOTTISH RIFLES.			OCTOBER, 1918.	
	15/18		Battalion remained at MALINCOURT training:- On 15th October Officers of Battalion Headquarters and in command of Companies with Signallers and Cyclists took part in a Brigade Exercise - Skeleton Scheme of Advanced Guards MALINCOURT - VILLERS OUTREAUX and outposts beyond latter village.	
	19		Battalion moved from MALINCOURT across country to TROISVILLES where it rested in billets till.	
	22		At 19 hours on this date the Battalion marched out to cross the SELLE River between MONTAY and NEUVILLY and continue the attack through RICHMONT and CROISETTE in conjunction with 21st DIVISION on the left and 98th Brigade on the right. Major O.G.SCOTT, M.C., took over command of the Battalion on leaving TROISVILLES. On arrival of the Battalion at the point of assembly which was the QUARRY N.W. of the Railway embankment a hot meal was served to the men and at 2400 hours C,D, and B Companies moved out to take up their position on the tape.	
	23		At 00.30 hours the enemy put down a very heavy barrage on and behind the assembly point which greatly disorganised the Battalion and caused fairly heavy casualties, C Company having two platoons practically wiped out. Nevertheless owing to the energy displayed by the Officers, and Sergeants in re-organisation the Battalion was able to move forward at ZERO,viz:. 02.00 hours,to the attack. The order of the Battalion was C Company on the right, D in the centre and B on the left. A Company was kept in Reserve in the QUARRY under the orders of the Battalion Commander. on the left the attack progressed very well but the right wing was soon held up by machine gun fire. This temporarily held up the right wing but it was eventually overcome by these German Machine Gun posts being outflanked. The left now continued very much in advance of the right until the first objective was reached and the pause of 40 minutes then enabled the right flank to come	

Army Form C. 2118.

WAR DIARY
or
INTELLIGENCE SUMMARY.
(Erase heading not required.)

Instructions regarding War Diaries and Intelligence Summaries are contained in F. S. Regs., Part II. and the Staff Manual respectively. Title pages will be prepared in manuscript.

Place	Date	Hour	Summary of Events and Information	Remarks and references to Appendices
1/6TH SCOTTISH RIFLES.			OCTOBER, 1918.	

| | 23 | | up and the line to be re:established. The first objective was reached at 03.40 hours and at 04.20 hours the barrage moved over with the advancing troops close behind. The left of the Battalion succeeded in getting through to the final objective arriving there at 06.30 hours. The right of the Battalion was held up by strong opposition in the vicinity of the SLAUGHTER HOUSE but this was eventually outflanked and overcome and the whole Battalion was on the final objective and consolidating the position at 07.00 hours. The number of officer casualties during the advance were 1 killed, and 6 wounded and 20 Other Ranks killed and 128 Other Ranks wounded. At this stage THE QUEENS and THE CAMERONIANS passed through the Battalion and continued the advance to VENDEGIES WOOD. The Battalion remained in the posts dug until night when orders were received that the advance would be continued on the following morning (24th) at 04.00 hours when the Battalion would pass through the CAMERONIANS outpost line. Four Field Guns, 2 Trench Mortars and 50 machine guns were captured during the day, also 197 prisoners were taken and 245 enemy dead counted. | |
| | 24 | | The Battalion after having had a hot meal fell in at 07.30 hours and moved down to the N.E. end of VENDEGIES WOOD, where they formed up in the following battle order :- A, B, C, D Companies from left to right. The K.O.Y.L.I. were on the left of the Battalion and the 1st Middlesex on the right. At ZERO (04.00 hours) the Battalion moved forward under a light barrage and met withstrong machine gun opposition on the first crest also some strong belts of wire. This was successfully overcome and the advance continued to the sunken road. Many prisoners and machine guns being captured on the way. Here a short pause was made to enable the left flank to get forward when the advance was continued and the village of WAGNONVILLE successfully taken. No serious opposition was met after this until the final objective was taken which was reached about 06.30 hours. Here the CAMERONIANS who were the supporting Battalion passed through to continue the attack but they were soon held up by heavy machine gun fire from | |

Army Form C. 2118.

WAR DIARY
or
INTELLIGENCE SUMMARY.
(Erase heading not required.)

Place	Date	Hour	Summary of Events and Information	Remarks and references to Appendices
5/6th Bn. SCOTTISH RIFLES.			OCTOBER, 1918.	
	24		ENGLEFONTAINE and remained more or less stationary all day. During the afternoon the Battalion deployed in the orchards S. of the ENGLEFONTAINE Road in order to support the advance of the CAMERONIANS but as they were unable to get forward our-occupied of their right flank no advance was made and when darkness set in the Battalion dug in on the line of the first objective with the exception of "D" company, which, not having any Officers or senior N.C.Os left was withdrawn into cellars in POIX DU NORD as Battalion reserve.	
			During the night the posts were heavily shelled by guns of all calibres including some gas shells.	
			Casualties during the day 2 Officers and 42 N.C.Os and men.	
			One big gun was taken by the Battalion in POIX DU NORD and 30 machine guns and 115 prisoners. 125 dead were counted on the field.	
	25		At dawn the posts occupied by the Battalion were subjected to a heavy barrage which continued more or less all day and when darkness came the Battalion got permission to withdraw into cellars in POIX DU NORD to save further casualties.	
			POIX DU NORD was shelled with heavy shells during the night but only 1 L/Cpl. was killed.	
	26		Battalion still in cellars, but at 08.00 hours A Company was ordered forward to support the 16th K. R. R. C. who had moved forward the previous night to beyond the TILLERIES. About 09.00 hours B Company was ordered forward to support the 9th H.L.I. at ENGLEFONTAINE. Both companies came under heavy artillery fire during this advance and 1 Officer and 4 other ranks were killed and 5 other ranks wounded.	
			At 16.00 hours A Company was relieved and rejoined the Battalion at POIX DU NORD and at 17.00 hours B Company was relieved by the 386th Div. Congratulations were received from GENERAL SIR H.S.PINNEY, K.C.B. - see appendices.	
			the MAIRIE OF ENGLEFONTAINE and GENERAL SHUTE. - see appendices.	Nos.2 & 3.
			at/	

Army Form C. 2118.

WAR DIARY
or
INTELLIGENCE SUMMARY.
(Erase heading not required.)

Instructions regarding War Diaries and Intelligence Summaries are contained in F.S. Regs., Part II. and the Staff Manual respectively. Title pages will be prepared in manuscript.

Place	Date	Hour	Summary of Events and Information	Remarks and references to Appendices
5/6th SCOTTISH RIFLES.			OCTOBER, 1918.	
	26	19.00	At 19.00 hours the whole Battalion left POIX DU NORD and marched back to FOREST where a hot meal was waiting and eventually continued the march to TROISVILLES where it went into rest billets arriving between 22 and 23.00 hours.	
	27		The Battalion rested and reorganised and part of the battalion was bathed.	
	28		Reorganisation was continued and the rest of the Battalion was bathed.	
	29		Lieut.-Col. H.B.SPENS, D.S.O., took over temporary command of the 19th Infantry Brigade.	
	30		The Commander of the V Corps (GENERAL SHUTE, C.B.,C.M.G.) inspected the 19th Infantry Brigade and addressed them on the recent operations. Afterwards the Battalions marched past and returned to billets. A copy of General SHUTE's address is appended vide Appendix No. 4.	No 4.
	31		Programme of training carried out in the vicinity of the village between 09.00 and 12.00 hours - Lewis Gun classes during the afternoon.	No.5.
			Programme of training carried out similar to the day before.	
			List of honors and awards vide appendix No 5.	

CASUALTIES FOR MONTH.

OFFICERS.
2/Lt. J.S. WATES, M.C. killed in action 23/10/18.
Lt. A.C. KERR   do.   26/10/18.
2/Lt. J. YOUNG   } wounded 23rd
"   D. FORD   } October
"   G. HIBBERT   } 1918.
"   W.A.G. PAULINGE }
"   W.McG. SMITH }
Lt. R. DICK   }

OTHER RANKS.
Killed in action 59
Wounded   196
Missing   5
Wounded at duty   5

Army Form C. 2118.

WAR DIARY
or
INTELLIGENCE SUMMARY.
(Erase heading not required.)

5/6TH SCOTTISH RIFLES.   Summary of Events and Information   OCTOBER, 1918.

CASUALTIES FOR MONTH Contd.

Officers.
Lieut. J.A.MACPHERSON, A.C. wounded 25th Octr.,1918
2/Lieut. A.ANDERSON   missing 24th Octr.,1918.

REINFORCEMENTS DURING MONTH.

Officers.	Other ranks.
Lieut.A.T.BAILLIE	102.

STRENGTH OF BATTALION.

Officers.	Other ranks.
28.	502.

[signature] Major,
Commanding 5/6th Bn. Scottish Rifles.

Place	Date	Hour		Remarks and references to Appendices

5/6TH SCOTTISH RIFLES.

WAR DIARY   OCTOBER, 1918.

APPENDIX No 1.

TRANSLATION.

CLARY. 11th October, 1918.

COMMUNE de CLARY.

To G.O.C.,
33rd Division.

In the name of the inhabitants whose sentiments I am happy to express, I beg respectfully to convey to you our admiration and keen and profound gratitude towards the valiant British troops, who with irresistable vigour have rolled back and driven out the barbarous invader whose yoke we have suffered for four long years.

Thanks to their rapid and vigourous pursuit the brave Scotch troops have succeeded in preventing the enemy from finishing the work of destruction he had commenced in our Commune. There has been no accident, no loss of life to deplore, our Church has been preserved to the last minute. The population during the last few days and hours which preceded their deliverance, have been able to resolutely resist the acts and threats of the German authorities. Their confidence has been as unshakeable as it was justified.

We offer our heartfelt gratitude to all the brave soldiers who have so generously poured out their blood in the sacred cause of right, justice and the independence of all peoples.

The valiant armies of the Allies, animated with a single spirit, a single will to conquer, will soon, we hope, have liberated all the invaded Provinces and have forced the barbarous monster to ask for mercy.

Honor and glory to them, eternal shame to the oppressor, source of so much woe and misery.

Will you kindly convey, Sir, to their Majesties, King George and his Gracious Queen Mary and to the Royal Family, the offering of our veneration and gratitude together with our warmest wishes for their happiness and the prosperity of the British Nation, now so closely bound to France in ties of brotherly love.

To your fine and warlike troops, who have shown themselves so kind and compassionate towards us, please present our kindest sympathy.

I have the honour to be,
Sir,
Yours respectfully,
(Signed) BONNEVILLE,
Maire de Clary.

5/6th SCOTTISH RIFLES.

WAR DIARY.   OCTOBER, 1918.

APPENDIX No. 2.

"C" Form.
MESSAGES AND SIGNALS.

Army Form C. 2123.
(.n books of 100.)

No. of Message ....

Prefix......Code......Words......	Received.	Sent, or sent out.	Office Stamp.
£ s. d.	From............	At ....m.	
Charges to Collect	By...............		
Service Instructions		To	
COPY.		By	

Handed in at..................................Office..........m. Received...........m.

TO FAJA

*Sender's Number.	Day of Month.	In reply to Number.	AAA
B.M.229	26		

following	received	from	div
begins	aaa	General	PINNEY
thanks	you	and	your
men	for	their	great
and	successful	efforts	

FROM

PLACE & TIME HASA

* This line should be erased if not required.

5/6TH SCOTTISH RIFLES.

WAR DIARY.   OCTOBER, 1918.

APPENDIX No. 3.

Copy.

TELEGRAM TO A.D.C. for G.O.C., 33rd DIVISION.

Sender's No.	Day of month.
140.	26/10/18.

MAIRE of ENGLEFONTAINE met this afternoon in a cellar of his village begs to express you in name of the 1200 inhabitants freed by the British Army his deepest feelings of hearty gratitude. I wish to add the best congratulations of the French Mission for the last night's most successful and brilliant operation.

From :- O.C. French Mission, 33rd Div.
                    (Signed   ) P. GIRARD, O.C.

TELEGRAM to G.O.C. 33rd DIVISION.

Sender's No.	Date.
G. 434	26.

    Please convey to all ranks under your command my congratulations on the gallantry and endurance they have shewn during the recent hard fighting. They may well be proud of the advance from MALINCOURT to the river SELLE where all resistance was overcome until the final objective was gained and the assault and capture of ENGLEFONTAINE with 500 Prisoners after 36 hours of continuous heavy fighting and hard marching over most difficult country was a gallant piece of work well organised and most gallantly carried out. The present nature of fighting was a little new to the Division which made their task harder and more costly yet, in spite of heavy casualties, their pluck, determination to win and splendid soldierlike spirit carried them through to success. Please convey to them my personal thanks for all they have done.

From :- General SHUTE.   Time :- 23.45.

5TH/6TH SCOTTISH RIFLES.

WAR DIARY.   OCTOBER, 1918.

APPENDIX No. 4.

Copy SPEECH delivered by GENERAL SHUTE, C.B., C.M.G.
Commander-in-Chief V Corps on the occasion of his
inspection of the 19th Infantry Brigade 29/10/18.

I want to congratulate you upon your work during the last few weeks - or month or two -. You have done well, jolly well, and the work has been frightfully hard.

Coming here as you did, at the moment I was almost afraid it might discourage you. You have had some very hard work and you have had some very long marches and the other day at ENGLEFONTAINE, I knew you were tired and about at the end of your tether and I asked you to do one bit more and you made a good show. It deserved enormous credit.

I knew you had not been doing open warfare until you came here and perhaps you were not quite as ready to take part in it as if you had been doing it longer. You found yourselves. You fought like the devil, and you know now you can fight and beat the Bosch whenever you can meet him. Remember there is not one of you men who cannot do in at least half a dozen bosches. Realise your strength and you will have success. If there is any hesitation about how good you are you will not succeed.

You will remember that some four or five months ago the Bosch said he had done in the English Army and at the time I said to some of my friends and some other people that he had not by any means.

This Brigade has an enormously strong record. But don't get into the way of thinking and living on the credit of people who preceded you. Remember we are all proud of our Brigade and of our Battalion, and if we are proud of them we must keep up the record they have made.

Now about the present situation of the war, you know we have been driving the Bosch back for a long while. You are fighting against an enemy getting used to defeat and I can tell you that when you fight him you will not be up against an enemy prepared to hold really strong positions. If we find that we shall have to attack with greater care. There is hardly a Division up against us now that has not been beaten at least twice. Everyone of the Bosch is only longing to desert or be taken prisoner. That is one of the reasons why we have been attacking him at night, because the German at night knows his Officers cannot see him and he can put his hands up and be taken prisoner, which he would not do during the day time. As a matter of fact there are no reserves behind them.

You have seen in your attacks they are scattered over the country in little batches with machine guns. These guns are well sighted and if you allow them to hold you up for a quarter of an hour, they will probably hold you up for a couple of hours. If you dash into them, or better still, go round them and flank them they give in. There is talk about peace and all of you have heard talk about peace. Politians may have their point of view. Remember that we have had four damned bad years and you have seen your friends killed and are we to stop when a few more rounds will knock him right out.

Be certain of yourselves. Be certain that you can beat the Bosch and remember we are near the last round, and remember we must knock him out. Always try to go round a position in preference to going straight at it. When you decide to go round get away at once.

We are getting near the end of the war and the prisoners we take now won't have very long to do work for us and remember we shall not get so much value from them. Kill the Germans so that they will not be able to come up against us again. Don't think

P.T.O.

think about anything else but knock the blighter out and see the end of it.

5TH/6TH SCOTTISH RIFLES.

WAR DIARY.   OCTOBER, 1918.

APPENDIX No. 5.

5TH/6TH SCOTTISH RIFLES.

HONORS and AWARDS.

AWARDED THE MILITARY CROSS :-
    Capt. STEWART, A.C.
    " CLARK, N. M.M.
    Lieut. MACPHERSON, J.H.
    2/Lt. MACDOUGALL, B.W.
    " CLARK, J.P.

AWARDED DISTINGUISHED CONDUCT MEDAL :-
    200894 Sgt. TAYLOR, M.

AWARDED BAR TO DISTINGUISHED CONDUCT MEDAL :-
    200545 C.S.M. HAY, J. D.C.M.,M.M.

AWARDED MEDAILLE MILITAIRE :-
    240026 R.Q.M.S. RENSHAW, H.

AWARDED THE MILITARY MEDAL :-
    9153 Rfm. CURTIS, H.
    38672 Sgt. SHAW, W.
    240134 " MILLER, J.
    200846 L/Sgt. HYSLOP, J.
    202297 Rfm. MCLAUGHLIN, H.
    42934 " JOHNSON, W.
    241312 " MITCHELL, A.
    31699 " SAMSON, W.
    42935 " STRACHAN, E.
    32106 " PITCAIRN, A.
    46221 " DAVIDSON, A.
    202859 " GRANT, W.
    56426 " KIRKWOOD, W.
    202345 Cpl. MUNNS, A.
    202791 Sgt. WIGHTMAN, W.
    238015 L/Cpl. SLOAN, R.
    202892 " CROUCH, J.H.
    202144 Sgt. LEES, C.
    291256 Cpl. KELLY, W.
    42692 Rfm. GIBSON, A.
    40809 " OLIVER, A.
    201428 " MCKENNA, W.
    41625 Cpl. KNOX, A.
    16501 Rfm. WALSH, A.
    202256 " MEE, G.
    291654 " FISHER, R.
    203903 " JOHNSTONE, C.G.
    241386 " FAWCETT, T.
    28462 L/Cpl. ROBERTSON, R.
    19898 Rfm. WIGLEY, J.
    266291 Sgt. REID, G.
    241679 Rfm. SIBBALD, H.
    202217 Cpl. LOCKHART, W.
    202274 Rfm. MCLURE, S.
    240251 Sgt. WATSON, A.
    200335 L/Cpl. HOUSTON, C.
    38096 Rfm. NIVEN, D.
    201668 L/Cpl. BELL, G.
    41675 " CAIRNIE, J.
    39802 Rfm. PARIS, D.
    39262 L/Cpl. AITKEN, A.
    42923 Rfm. RUDDIMAN, G.

AWARDED BAR TO THE MILITARY MEDAL :-
    291137 Sgt. MORRISON, J. M.M.
    200846 L/Cpl. DOBBIE, J. M.M.
    202467 Sgt. BELL, J. M.M.
    202345 Cpl. MUNNS, A. M.M.

AWARDED MERITORIOUS SERVICE MEDAL :-
    266384 Sgt. McDONALD, R.S.

Army Form C. 2118.

WAR DIARY
or
INTELLIGENCE SUMMARY.
(Erase heading not required.)

5TH SCOTTISH RIFLES.   Summary of Events and Information   **NOVEMBER, 1918.**

Place	Date	Hour	Summary of Events and Information	Remarks and references to Appendices
TROISVILLES	1		Battalion in rest billets at TROISVILLE. During the morning training programme carried out in the vicinity of the village. A draft of 49 N.C.Os. and men joined the Battalion during the morning chiefly from the 4th Battalion from REDFORD BARRACKS. During the Afternoon the Commanding Officer (Major C.O. SCOTT, M.C.) inspected the Transport - "D" Company's cooker especially commended for its smartness. In the evening at 17.45 hours the Battalion paraded and carried out a night marching scheme on compass bearings.	
	2		The Battalion carried out a scheme near AUDENCOURT. "A", "B", and "C" Companies being attacking force and "D" Company the defending force.	
	3		Church parade at 11.30 hours after which the Commanding Officer visited the billets.	
ENGLEFONTAINE	4		The Battalion with the rest of the Brigade left TROISVILLES and marched to ENGLEFONTAINE bivouacing in Orchards there for the night.	
MORMAL FOREST	5		The Battalion with the rest of the Brigade left ENGLEFONTAINE in the early morning and passed through the Forest of MORMAL halting 1½ kilometres S.W. of SARBARAS where the Brigade bivouaced and remained during the night in Divisional Reserve. Very wet day and night.	
AULNOYE.	6		Bridgeheads across the SAMBRE River were established by the leading Brigades before dawn. The Battalion was ordered forward to pass through the 98th Brigade and attack LE BOUVIER and AULNOYE STATION, The CAMERONIANS advancing on the right through Petit MAUBEUGE; 1st Queens Regiment in support. At 13.40 hours we had captured AULNOYE STATION practically without resistance except for severe harassing fire from the enemy's rearguard artillery. Finally the Companies took up positions as follows :- "A" Company facing N.E. North of Village near Brickfield. Remaining three Companies along Crest E. of village. In this operation Capt. R. DOWNIE, M.C., D.C.M. was killed and 2/Lieut. F. SUNTER	

Army Form C. 2118.

WAR DIARY
or
INTELLIGENCE SUMMARY.
(Erase heading not required)

Instructions regarding War Diaries and Intelligence Summaries are contained in F.S. Regs., Part II. and the Staff Manual respectively. Title pages will be prepared in manuscript.

Place	Date	Hour	Summary of Events and Information	Remarks and references to Appendices
			5/TH SCOTTISH RIFLES. NOVEMBER, 1918.	
ECUELIN	6		M.C. was wounded. Casualties amongst other ranks amounted to 12. Another very wet day and weather conditions as bad as they possibly could be.	
	7		At 05.45 hours in conjunction with the 21st Division on our left and The CAMERONIANS on the right, the advance was continued Eastwards without definite artillery support, and under difficult weather conditions as a heavy mist prevailed throughout the day so that direction and touch with flanking units was not easily maintained. At this stage men were suffering from the heavy rain and continual exposure in the open without any opportunity of drying themselves. Until our men reached EUGELIN no opposition was encountered but once there heavy shell fire was opened. The enemy had left small parties in the village who were quickly overcome. Progress, however, was impeded by heavy machine gun fire mainly from the left flank and edge of LIMONT FONTAINE which was in possession of the enemy till the end of the day. Numerous Machine Guns defended the N.W. edge of BOIS du TEMPLE and the enemy was still able to harass the village of ECUELIN and its approaches by heavy bursts of artillery and trench mortar fire. Eventually a line was established outside the E. edge of ECUELIN, the Company on the left penetrating to a sunken road N of the wood, where they captured a machine gun and killed the crew. The enemy's flank S of BOIS du TEMPLE was turned before nightfall and shortly afterwards the enemy's resistance on the front broke down and the left flank division pressed forward as far as EGLAIBES. About 10 p.m. the 13th and 14th WELCH Regiments proceeded to LE TOQUE where hot soup was issued from the Field Cookers and the Battalion rested till dawn. After relief Companies marched to LE TOQUE to take over the Battalion Sector. Our casualties in this operation were :- Capt. N. CLARK, M.C. M.M. wounded. Other ranks 20 killed, wounded and missing.	
SARBARAS.	8		At 06.30 hours the Battalion proceeded from LE TOQUE and marched to SARBARAS where billets were allotted. The remainder of the day was given over to cleaning and drying of clothing equipment and arms.	

Army Form C. 2118.

WAR DIARY
or
INTELLIGENCE SUMMARY.
(Erase heading not required.)

Instructions regarding War Diaries and Intelligence Summaries are contained in F. S. Regs., Part II. and the Staff Manual respectively. Title pages will be prepared in manuscript.

5TH SCOTTISH RIFLES.   Summary of Events and Information   NOVEMBER, 1918.

Place	Date	Hour	Summary of Events and Information	Remarks and references to Appendices
S ARBARAS	8		BRIGADE COMMANDER The following message from MAJOR GENERAL SIR R.J.PINNEY to the Brigadier General was communicated to all Battalions :- "Hearty congratulations on fine work carried out by you and your Brigade during the battle of SAMBRE, Novr. 5th, 6th and 7th".	
	9		Battalion rested and carried on with cleaning up. Special Order of the day by Field Marshal SIR DOUGLAS HAIG received with reference to the operations at POIX du NORD on 28th Octr.. see Appendix No 1.	1
	10		Church parade at 11.30 hours.	
	11		News of the signing of the Armistice received early in the morning saying hostilities would cease at 11 hoursand no intercourse was to be held with the enemy. Letter "B" Company inspected at 10 hours in marching order by the Commanding Officer. A draft of four officers and 139 Other ranks arrived to join the Battalion.	
	12		At 13.30 hours the Battalion paraded and marched to BERLAIMONT and took over billets there occupied by the 12th MANCHESTER REGIMENT. A message was received from G.O.C. V Corps for copy of which see appendix No 2.	2
	13		Battalion paraded at 9 hours and marched to field in rear of Battalion Headquarters where the Companies carried out close order drill under company arrangements until 12 hours. Lieut.-Colonel H.B.SPENS, D.S.O. in temporary command of the 19th Infantry Brigade inspected the new draft at 10 hours. During the afternoon the Divisional Baths were allotted to the Battalion.	

Army Form C. 2118.

WAR DIARY
or
INTELLIGENCE SUMMARY.
(Erase heading not required.)

5TH SCOTTISH RIFLES.   Summary of Events and Information   NOVEMBER, 1918.

Place	Date	Hour	Summary of Events and Information	Remarks and references to Appendices
SARBARAS	14		The Commanding Officer inspected each Company in the Battalion in marching order during the morning. At 12 hours all Officers and N.C.Os. attended a lecture in the 21st Division Theatre on "DEMOBILIZATION" by Lieut. McLAREN, A.S.C. The Brigadier General 19th Infantry Brigade returned from leave and took over command of brigade from Lieut.-Colonel H.B.SPENS, D.S.O. who resumed thereupon the command of the battalion.	
LOC QUIGNOL	15		The Battalion paraded at 10.00 hours and with the rest of the Brigade marched to LOC QUIGNOL where it remained billetted for the night partly in houses and barns and half of "D" Company and the Headquarter Details in tents.	
LOC QUIGNOL to CROIX	16		The Battalion left LOC QUIGNOL at 08.30 hours and marched via ENGLEFONTAINE to CROIX where it was billetted for the night in empty and ruined houses.	
CLARY	17		The Battalion left CROIX at 08.20 hours and marched via MONTAY and TROISVILLES and BERTRY to CLARY, where it was accommodated in billets with the remainder of the 19th Infantry Brigade.	
	18		The Battalion paraded at 10.00 hours in the field East of the village and carried out Battalion Drill under the C.O. until 11 hours when the Companies were handed over to Company Officers Commanders for an hours drill under Company arrangements. Classes for N.C.Os held during the afternoon.	
	19		Battalion drill under the Commanding Officer from 09.00 to 10.00 hours, after which Companies drilled under their Company Commanders until 13.30 hours. The Brigadier General inspected all the billets of the Battalion at 11.30 hours.	

WAR DIARY
or
INTELLIGENCE SUMMARY.

(Erase heading not required.)

Army Form C. 2118.

Place	Date	Hour	Summary of Events and Information	Remarks and references to Appendices
CLARY			5TH SCOTTISH RIFLES. NOVEMBER, 1918.	
	19		"A" Company played "B" Company at football in the afternoon and "C" Company played "D".	
	20		Battalion drill under the Commanding officer from 08.00 hours to 10.00 hours after which Companies drilled under their Company Commanders till 12.30 hours. At 14.30 hours the Commanding Officer inspected the Transport.	
	21		Companies drilled under their Company Commanders during the morning and in turn went to the Baths in the Square where after bathing each man got a complete change of underclothing. At 11.30 hours the Brigadier inspected the Battalion Transport in a field behind the Transport Billet - "D" Company especially commended for the turn out of their cooker.	
	22		Battalion drill under the Commanding Officer for the first hour of the morning parade after which Company Commanders carried out with Company training.	
	23		Owing to the cold weather, no Battalion drill was carried out and Companies carried on training under Company arrangements.	
	24		A Thanksgiving and Memorial Service was held by the 19th Infantry Brigade in a field East of CLARY for all denominations which the Battalion attended in the morning at 11.30 hours. The Brigadier addressed the troops at the opening of the service and at the conclusion. The Brigade including the 11th Field Company R.E. No3 Company Train A.S.C. and the 19th Field Ambulance marched past the Brigadier in course of route leaving the field. The Divisional Band played the hymns at the service which was conducted by the Revd. W.C.MAYNE Senior C. of E. PADRE of the Division assisted by Revd. S.O.STEWART the Padre attached to the Battalion.	

Army Form C. 2118.

WAR DIARY
or
INTELLIGENCE SUMMARY.
(Erase heading not required.)

Place	Date	Hour	Summary of Events and Information	Remarks and references to Appendices

5TH SCOTTISH RIFLES. NOVEMBER, 1918.

Place	Date	Hour	Summary of Events and Information	Remarks
CLARY	25		The Brigade Route March was cancelled owing to the wet morning and Companies carried on training in and in the vicinity of their billets. A telegram of congratulation was received from the Territorial Force Association GLASGOW during the morning (see appendix No 3.) to which the Commanding Officer sent a reply of thanks (Appendix No 4) At 17.00 hours a Battalion Concert was held in the Cinema House CLARY assisted by the Band of the 101st Field Ambulance. The entertainment lasted 2½ hours and was a great success, the hall being packed.	3 4
	26		The Battalion paraded at 08.30 hours and proceeded to an area near CLARY where salving operations over the old battle fields were carried out resulting in a large quantity of material of various kinds being brought in. The Battalion returned to billets at 12.30 hours. At 14.50 hours a lecture on "DEMOBILIZATION" was given by Revd. STEWART KENNEDY in the Recreation Room near CLARY Church which was largely attended.	
	27		Battalion drill under Commanding Officer in the morning for an hour, after which Companies carried out drill under Company Commanders. Educational Scheme started. Classes held from 11.30 to 12.30 hours in elementary subjects. At 14.30 hours Transport Competition for prizes given by Lieut.-Colonel SPENS, D.S.O., was held in field near Transport Lines :- Best Cooker :- "D" Company. Lewis Gun Limber :- "C" Company. Other vehicle :- No 2 Water Cart. Pack pony :- "Jess" Mule. The Judges were Cookers and L.G.Limbers :- Brigadier General C.K.B Mayne, D.S.O. and Capt J.E.C.Hay, Staff Captain. Pack ponies and other vehicles :- Lieut.-Colonel H.C. Hyde Smith D.S.O. and Capt Morie, 1st Cameronians.	

Army Form C. 2118.

WAR DIARY
or
INTELLIGENCE SUMMARY.
(Erase heading not required.)

Instructions regarding War Diaries and Intelligence Summaries are contained in F. S. Regs., Part II. and the Staff Manual respectively. Title pages will be prepared in manuscript.

Place	Date	Hour	Summary of Events and Information	Remarks and references to Appendices
5TH SCOTTISH RIFLES.			NOVEMBER, 1918.	
CLARY.	28		Training was carried out during the morning under Company arrangements and under the supervision of second in Command of Companies All Company Commanders being occupied working out papers etc for draft of 73 Miners in the Battalion to be released immediately to their trade. Educational classes as usual between 11.30 and 12.30 hours. Letter of congratulation received from Lieut.-Colonel R.M. BENZIE, Senior Lieut.-Colonel of 5th Scottish Rifles, see appendix No 5.	5
	29		The draft of 73 Miners headed by the Pipe Band of the Battalion left for MONTIGNY at 08.00 hours and was seen off by Brigadier General C.R.S. MAYNE, D.S.O. and Lieut.-Colonel H.B.SPENS, D.S.O. at 9.30 hours. The Battalion paraded in Marching Order ~~front MONTIGNY~~ went for a route march, the route taken being MONTIGNY - LIGNY-en-CAMBRESIS - CAULLERY and then back to CLARY. Lecture on the Water Cart by the Medical Officer during the afternoon and one on the Field Kitchen by the Master Cook also in the afternoon.	
	30		ST ANDREW'S DAY. 19 more Coal-miners left the Battalion at 09.00 hours for MONTIGNY en route for Scotland to return tom their employment. The Battalion paraded at 09.00 hours and carried out drill on the parade ground under the Company Commanders. In the afternoon the Battalion played the Cameronians at Football and were beaten by 3 goals to 2. In the evening the officers held their ST ANDREW'S night dinner at the Headquarter's Mess in the Square and the Pipe Band played during the dinner.	6

List of honours and awards see Appendix No 6.

CASUALTIES FOR MONTH.

Army Form C. 2118.

WAR DIARY
or
INTELLIGENCE SUMMARY.
(Erase heading not required).

5TH SCOTTISH RIFLES.   Summary of Events and Information   **NOVEMBER, 1918.**

CASUALTIES FOR MONTH.

OFFICERS.   **OTHER RANKS.**

Capt. R. DOWNIE, M.C.,D.C.M. killed 6/11/18.   Killed in action 1
2/Lieut. F. SUMTER, M.C. wounded 6/11/18.   Wounded 20.
Capt. N. CLARK, M.C.,M.M. " 7/11/18.
Lieut. W.V. PARK wounded 7/11/18.

REINFORCEMENTS FOR MONTH.

2/Lieut. R.S.L. SMITH.
Lieut.   A.   WATSON.
Lieut.   M.   BLAIR.
Lieut.   R.   CAMERON.   Other Ranks 242.
Lieut.   A.G. LAWSON.
2/Lieut. C.J. HOOLEY.
Lieut.   A. McL. CRAWFORD.
2/Lieut. G. HARDIE.

STRENGTH OF BATTALION.

Officers. 34   Other Ranks. 651.

Hugh B. Spens
Lieut.-Colonel,
Commanding 5th Battalion Scottish

Place	Date	Hour		Remarks and references to Appendices

Instructions regarding War Diaries and Intelligence Summaries are contained in F.S. Regs. Part II. and the Staff Manual respectively. Title pages will be prepared in manuscript.

/5th Battalion Scottish Rifles.

War Diary — November 1918.

Appendix No. 1.

Army Form C. 2118.

WAR DIARY
or
INTELLIGENCE SUMMARY.

(Erase heading not required.)

Place	Date	Hour	Summary of Events and Information	Remarks and references to Appendices
5th Scottish Rifles			November 1918	
			Appendix No. 1.	
			Special Orders of the day by Field Marshall Sir Douglas Haig KT, G.C.B, G.C.V.O., K.C.I.E. Commander-in-Chief, British Armies in France.	
			The following message, which was handed to the General Officer Commanding, 19th Infantry Brigade by an inhabitant of Pont-du-Nord on the 26th October 1918, is published for the information of all ranks:-	
			(Translation)	
			To the Commander-in-Chief of the British Armies in France, and the Officers and Soldiers.	
			It is with a feeling of patriotic gratitude that the population of Pont-du-Nord greet their brave brothers-in-arms, the British troops.	
			This gratitude will be eternal, for French hearts will never forget the gallantry and the sacrifices made by the British troops fighting side by side with French soldiers for the deliverance of the part of France from the yoke of the barbarians.	
			All those, of every degree, from General to private soldier, have fought for this noble cause of justice and the liberty of the world, and merit immortality.	

Army Form C. 2118.

WAR DIARY
or
INTELLIGENCE SUMMARY.
(Erase heading not required.)

Instructions regarding War Diaries and Intelligence Summaries are contained in F. S. Regs., Part II. and the Staff Manual respectively. Title pages will be prepared in manuscript.

Place	Date	Hour	Summary of Events and Information	Remarks and references to Appendices
5th Scottish Rifles			Appendix No.	November, 1918.

I am glad, in spite of my misery, that my four sons have fought with you for a great ideal. And I would point out, above all, that if you show pity to the little ones (I speak of the simple soldiers unconscious of the evil that they have done, the character they have shown under the lies of their superiors, and the hatred that they have inculcated against their superiors) do not show it to the chiefs, to the scoundrels who, for the sole purpose of dominating the world, and to enslave the people, are responsible for the deaths of many millions of honest sons, and to enslave the people, are responsible for the deaths of many millions of honest

You murdered and ruined France, for England, for our sisters of America, of Italy, of Belgium, of Portugal, of Serbia, of Montenegro, of Roumania, and of all the photo of the civilised world. I wish to pay, punish the great criminal Wilhelm, the responsible author of all the assassinations, violations and ruins.

In order that this war shall be the last, Noble Allies, you must go to Berlin and to Vienna, and unfurl the flag of the League of Nations. It reflects in its folds the triumph of justice and liberty of the people over despotisms and barbarity.

In your courage, when you head in your turn on the soil of the enemy country, you will respect the women and the children, and the aged; you will show the world that you are not an army of assassins as the great army which is coming down.

A6945 Wt. W14122/M1160 350,000 12/16 D. D. & L. Forms/C./2118/14.

Army Form C. 2118.

WAR DIARY
or
INTELLIGENCE SUMMARY.
(Erase heading not required.)

Place	Date	Hour	Summary of Events and Information	Remarks and references to Appendices
5th Scottish Rifles			Appendix No 1 Continued. November 1918	

"When this conduct will lead to the repentance of the German women, to the end that they will bring up their sons in a saner education.

English people, you have merited, with all the Allies, the gratitude of humanity.

Allied brothers, thank you for our deliverance.

Be kind enough to testify, for this grand act in history, to your noble Sovereign and his gracious family, all the gratitude of the women, the aged, and the children of the martyred provinces."

Bois du Nord. 24th October, 1918.
                                    (Signed) Louis Ykafram.
(Written inside the fire of the deliverance)

                                    (Signed) D. Haig Y.M.
                                    Commander-in-Chief
                                    British Armies in France

General Headquarters
7th November, 1918.

5th Battalion Scottish Rifles.

War Diary — November, 1918.

Appendix No 2.

Army Form C. 2118.

WAR DIARY
or
INTELLIGENCE SUMMARY.
(Erase heading not required.)

Instructions regarding War Diaries and Intelligence Summaries are contained in F. S. Regs., Part II. and the Staff Manual respectively. Title pages will be prepared in manuscript.

Place	Date	Hour	Summary of Events and Information	Remarks and references to Appendices
5th Scottish Rifles			November, 1918.	
			Appendix No 2	
Officer Commanding				BM 273.
1st Queens				
1st Cameronians				
5th L.N. Rifles				
19th T.M. Bty			The following message from G.O.C. V Corps, is published for the information of all ranks :—	
			"On the signature of the Armistice, I wish to convey to all ranks of the V Corps, my most sincere & cordial Congratulations on the gallantry and endurance AAA No task has been too arduous for you AAA No difficulty too great for you to surmount AAA The prominent part taken by the V Corps in the defeat of the enemy has only been rendered possible by the gallant and unselfish manner in which every Officer, NCO and man in the Corps has played up for the common good AAA The command of such troops has been an honour for me, which I shall always remember."	
			(Sd.) L General C. D. Shute.	
	11/11/18			
	12/11/18		(Sd) T.J. Little, Lieut. for Captain, Brigade Major 19th Infantry Brigade	

5th Battalion Scottish Rifles

War Diary — November, 1918.

Appendix No 3.

Honours and Awards

Bar to the Military Cross

Capt. A C Stewart M.C.
2/Lieut. F. Sunter M.C.

The Military Cross

Capt. C. E. Grant
Lieut. A. R. Paxton.

The Distinguished Conduct Medal

240081 C S M Stevenson J MM
200404 Sergt Logie R.
202791   "   Wightman W MM

Bar to the Military Medal

241419 Sgt Gallacher J MM

Military Medal

23026	L/Cpl	Selkirk	A B	41205	Sgt	Crum W
200756	Rfm	McPhee	M	34567	Rfm	Wheatley R
28379	"	Mochan	J	240921	"	Anderson A
267073	L/Cpl	Younns	A	33686	"	Baker H
202301	Rfm	Brown	D	202776	"	Glen W. J
242103	"	Turner	G	35015	"	Reid J
27795	"	Smith	D	53085	"	Wotherspoon J
56439	"	Robertson	R	38420	L/Cpl	Nicholson N
16229	L/Cpl	Crowe	W	34551	Rfm	Johnson J.R
240022	Sgt	Burt J	AM	202377	Cpl	Donald P.W
202948	Rfm	Tebbs	J	238110	Rfm	Scott W
241352	"	Ainley	H	200529	Cpl	Watt G
		40479	Rfm	Armitage W		

5th Battalion Scottish Rifles.

War Diary. November, 1918.

Appendix No 4.

5th Battalion Scottish Rifles

War Diary — November 1918.

Appendix No. 6.

"A" Form
MESSAGES AND SIGNALS.

Army Form C. 2121 (in pads of 100)

No. of Message..............

Prefix........... Code........... m
Office of Origin and Service Instructions

A411 C 6H 24
PM GLASGOW
L OHMS 25

Words. | Charge.
Sent
At.................m
To.................
By.................

This message is on a/c of:
.... Service.
(Signature of "Franking Officer.")

Recd. at............m
Date.................
From.................
By.................

TO OFFICER COMMANDING 1/5TH SCOTTISH RIFLES FRANCE

Sender's Number. | Day of Month. | In reply to Number. | AAA

HEARTIEST CONGRATULATIONS TO YOU AND TO ALL RANKS ON THE SPLENDID RESULT OF YOUR EFFORTS

From GLASGOW TERRITORIAL FORCE ASSOCIATION
Place
Time

The above may be forwarded as now corrected. (Z)

Censor. | Signature of Addressee or person authorised to telegraph in his name.
* This line should be erased if not required.

"A" Form
MESSAGES AND SIGNALS.

Army Form C. 2121
(In pads of 100)
No. of Message..............

Prefix........ Code............m	Words.	Charge.	This message is on a/c of:	Recd. at.........m
Office of Origin and Service Instructions		Sent		Date................
....	At...............m		.....................Service.	From.................
....	To.................		(Signature of "Franking Officer.")	By....................
....	By................			

TO | GLASGOW T.F. ASSOCN

| Sender's Number. | Day of Month. | In reply to Number. | AAA |
| * J 104 | 25 | | |

ALL	RANKS	ARE	PROUD
TO	RECEIVE	YOUR	CONGRATULATIONS
AND	THANK	YOU	FOR
THEM			

From 5TH   SCOTTISH RIFLES
Place
Time

(Sgd) Hugh B. Spens
Lt. Col.
Signature of Addressor or person authorised to telegraph in his name.

* This line should be erased if not required.

5th Battalion Scottish Rifles.

War Diary. November, 1918.

Appendix No 5.

Army Form C. 2118.

WAR DIARY
or
INTELLIGENCE SUMMARY.
(Erase heading not required.)

5th Scottish Rifles Appendix No 5   November 1918.

Northern District Headquarters
(Irish Command)
Belfast. 11th November, 1918

To Lt Colonel A.B. Shaw D.S.O.
Comdg 15th Scottish Rifles B.E.F.

My dear Colonel,

On the cessation of hostilities, I hasten to congratulate you, and the Officers, N.C.O.s and men who have, during the long periods of the war, so well and so worthily upheld the honour and traditions of the old Battalion, and who by untiring zeal and courage during a period of long trial have taken your full share in the glorious conflict which has just been brought to such a successful termination.

Although I am not at the moment in personal touch with them, I know that every Officer and man of the 5th Scottish Rifles (scattered as they are at present in the four areas of the earth) joins with me in thanking you and those under your command for so gallantly keeping the honour and name of the Battalion alive, and in expressing our gratitude and heartfelt thanks to you

WAR DIARY
or
INTELLIGENCE SUMMARY.
(Erase heading not required.)

Army Form C. 2118.

Place	Date	Hour	Summary of Events and Information	Remarks and references to Appendices
5th Scottish Rifles	November 1918		Affectionately just and	

all for your great sacrifices in this great and glorious war.

Needless to say that friendship (leisure) to the occasion which will permit me to summons together from all quarters the Officers and men of the 5th Scottish Rifles in order to place on record my undying gratitude and thanks to the Officers, Non-Commissioned Officers and men who comprised the 5th Scottish Rifles in the field at the termination of hostilities.

I also take the present opportunity of conveying to you my personal gratification and congratulations on the honours and distinctions conferred on you for your heroic leadership and personal bravery during your command of the Battalion in the Field.

All honour to you and to your Officers, N.C.Os and men for their heroic part in the great European War.

With all good wishes

I am,

my dear Colonel

Yours sincerely

(Sgd) H. M. Bengie Lt. Colonel

5th Scottish Rifles

WAR DIARY
or
INTELLIGENCE SUMMARY

Army Form C. 2118.

WO 50

Place	Date	Hour	Summary of Events and Information	Remarks and references to Appendices
5?/6th Leather? Rifles	1		Battalion at CLARY. Church Parade under Revd. H. Brown Senior C. of E. Chaplain in the 33rd Division, in the Cinema Hall at 10.15 hours	
	2		A draft of 58 men left for the U.K. to resume their employment. Brigade Ceremonial Parade on the Battalion Parade Ground under command of the Brigadier	
	3		Brigade Route March at OG 30 hours route CLARY - CAULLERY - LIGNY-EN-CAMBRESIS - MONTIGNY and thence back to CLARY	
	4		The King and his suite arrived in CLARY about 12.40 hours and halted in the Place des Ecrivais for ten minutes. The Battalion turned out on the Place and this Battalions lined part of the route. The inhabitants made a good display of bunting and on two large canvases of either side of the square suspended across the street the following greetings were painted in bold letters :- "GLOIRE et HONNEUR à NOS LIBERATEURS" "HOMAGE à la NATION ANGLAISE". The King was accompanied	

WAR DIARY
or
INTELLIGENCE SUMMARY.
(Erase heading not required.)

Army Form C. 2118.

Place	Date	Hour	Summary of Events and Information	Remarks and references to Appendices
	5/6th Scottish Rifles		December 1918.	

by the Prince of Wales and as soon as they appeared they were loudly cheered by the troops and civilians. On stepping from the car His Majesty was met by Brig. General Baird, C.M.G., D.S.O. (acting Divisional Commander in the absence of Major-Gen. R.J. Pinney K.C.B.) An address of welcome was then read by one of the girls of the town and a bouquet of flowers was presented to His Majesty, who afterwards shook hands with the three inhabitants to whom New Duties had been entrusted. W.O. Maire and the Town Council were next introduced, An address by the Mayor (for translation of which see appendix I) not having been read at this moment was afterwards forwarded by Brigade to the proper quarter. Brig. General E.R.T. Wagner, D.S.O. was presented with others. His Majesty having asked to see the Colonel of the Battalion conversed with Lt.Col. W.B. Spens D.S.O. for a few minutes and showed a keen interest in what took place on the day the Battalion captured the town. 1.

Army Form C. 2118.

WAR DIARY
or
INTELLIGENCE SUMMARY.
(Erase heading not required.)

Place	Date	Hour	Summary of Events and Information	Remarks and references to Appendices
5/6th Scottish Rifles			December 1918.	
	4.		Sunday. Scenes of great enthusiasm. The King and the Prince of Wales entered their Car again at the time appointed and proceeded along the road to MOTTIGNY.	
	5.		The Companies drilled under their Company Commanders during the morning and Educational Classes were held as usual. The Brigadier General visited the Educational Classes of the Battalion at 11.30 hours and later inspected the Regimental Workshops at 11.30 hours and later inspected the Regimental Workshops at 09.15 hours. At 11.30 hours Brigade Route March commenced.	
	6.		The Battalion Transport was inspected by Colonel Dee, C.M.G., D.S.O. Commanding the Divisional Base.	
	7.		Companies drilled under their Company Commanders during the morning and the Lewis Gunners of "A" and "B" Companies fired on the Range. Educational Classes held at 11.30 hours. In the afternoon the Battalion football team played a friendly match versus the 1st Queens Regt. beating them by 3 goals to nil.	
	8.			

Army Form C. 2118.

Army Form C. 2118.

WAR DIARY
or
INTELLIGENCE SUMMARY.
(Erase heading not required.)

Place	Date	Hour	Summary of Events and Information	Remarks and references to Appendices
5/6th Scottish Rifles			December 1918	IV
	8.		Church Parade at 11.00 hours.	
	9.		Lt. Colonel H.B. Spens D.S.O. proceeded on leave to PARIS and Major C.E. Scott M.C. assumed command of the Battalion. Training took about.	
	10.		Classes as usual. Training as usual	
	11.		The 19th Infantry Brigade started their march to the AUNOIT area leaving CLARY at 0900 hours. The 5th Scottish Rifles being leading Battalion. — The Route taken was via LIGNY-HAUCOURT-ESNES-LESDAIN — CREVE COEUR (where the Brigade halted from 11.50 hours to 13.00 hours for dinner) After dinner the march was resumed to MASNIERES where the Brigade halted for the night. The Battalion was billeted in two saw houses on the MARCOING road. The Officers being on huts close by. The day was unfortunately most fearfully wet. The Divisional General saw the Brigade pass near LESDAIN —	
	12.		The march was resumed at 0900 hours the 1st Queens leading followed by the 2nd Camerons and the 5th Scottish Rifles marching third	

A6945 Wt. W14421/M1160 350,000 12/16 D. D. & L. Forms/C/2118/14.

Army Form C. 2118.

WAR DIARY
or
INTELLIGENCE SUMMARY.
(Erase heading not required.)

Remarks and references to Appendices: I

Place	Date	Hour	Summary of Events and Information
5/6th Scottish Rifles			December 1918.
			first and the rear Battalion being the 18th Middlesex (Pioneer) Regt.
			attached to the 19th Infantry Brigade for the whole period of the
			march. Wretched weather was experienced, heavy rain falling
			the whole day. The Route for the days march being MARCOING
			- RIBECOURT - HAVRINCOURT to HERMIES where the Brigade halted for
			the night and was accommodated in camps (tents) either side of
			the village.
	13		After a very dreary night in camp the march was continued
			at 9.00 hours. The 1st Cameronians leading and the 5th Scottish Rifles
			marching second. After passing through DOIGNIES the Route was
			BEAUMETZ-LES-CAMBRAI,— VELU and the LEBUCQUIÈRE to FRÉMICOURT
			where the Brigade halted for dinner. After dinner the march
			was continued to FAVREUIL where the Brigade halted for the night
			and were accommodated in wooden huts.
	14		The Brigade left FAVREUIL the 5th Scottish Rifles leading & passing
BAPAUME			the starting point (the monument commemorating the SAPIGNIES-

A6945 Wt. W1422/M160 350,000 12/16 D. D. & L. Forms/C./2118/14.

WAR DIARY or INTELLIGENCE SUMMARY

Army Form C. 2118.

Place	Date	Hour	Summary of Events and Information	Remarks and references to Appendices
5th/6th Scottish Rifles			December 1918.	
			BAPAUME (Road) at 08.25 hours – The Route was via BAPAUME and the BAPAUME Road passing through WALENCOURT – LE SARS – POZIERES to near ALBERT. A halt was given from 11.50 hours to 13.00 hours for dinner? near POZIERES. On arrival at ALBERT the Battalion marched through it and was accommodated in a camp west of the town.	
	15		The Brigade left the camps outside ALBERT at 09.00 hours – The 5th Br. Scottish Rifles being the last Battalion to move. A halt was made near FRANVILLERS for dinner from 11.50 hours to 13.00 hours. The Brigade was billeted in the QUERRIEU area for the night, this Battalion being billeted LA HOUSSOYE.	
	16		The Battalion left LA HOUSSOYE at 08.00 hours and joined the Camerons and Brigade H.Q. at QUERRIEU. The 1st Queens and 15th Middlesex marching independently. A halt was made in the outskirts of AMIENS at 11.35 hours and the Battalion had dinner and then marched off again at 12.45 hours passing through AMIENS and reaching LONGPRE-LES-AMIENS at 13.45 hours.	

Army Form C. 2118.

WAR DIARY
or
INTELLIGENCE SUMMARY.
(Erase heading not required.)

Instructions regarding War Diaries and Intelligence Summaries are contained in F. S. Regs., Part II. and the Staff Manual respectively. Title pages will be prepared in manuscript.

Place	Date	Hour	Summary of Events and Information	Remarks and references to Appendices
5th/6th Scottish Rifles			December 1918.	VII
	17	10h00	where it remained the night in billets.	
			The Battalion left LONGPRÉ-LES-AMIENS at 09.10 hours in heavy rain and marched independantly to the rest of the Brigade. The route taken was through MONTIÈRES – DREUIL-LES-AMIENS – AILLY-SUR-SOMME to BREILLY where the main road was left. The Battalion halted for dinner just outside FOURDRINOY from 11.50 hours to 1300 hours and then marched on via in the afternoon through CAVILLOT and RIENCOURT just east of MONTAGNE. Major General O.C. R.Q. Pinney. K.C.B. D.S.O. The Battalion march past him and congratulated them on their appearance after so long a march under such inclemable weather conditions. On reaching MONTAGNE Battalion Headquarters and "A" & "B" Companies billeted here and "C" & "D" Companies proceeded to AVELESGES to billed there. Lt Col H.B. Spens DSO. returned from leave and resumed command of the Battalion.	
	18		Battalion rested and cleaned up.	
	19	10h00	"C" & "D" Companies left AVELESGES and marched to MONTAGNE where	

Army Form C. 2118.

WAR DIARY
or
INTELLIGENCE SUMMARY.
(Erase heading not required.)

Instructions regarding War Diaries and Intelligence Summaries are contained in F. S. Regs., Part II. and the Staff Manual respectively. Title pages will be prepared in manuscript.

Remarks and references to Appendices VIII

Place	Date	Hour	Summary of Events and Information	Remarks and references to Appendices
5/6th Scottish Rifles			December 1918.	
			whose billets had been found for "C" Company - "D" Company proceeded on to the village of LE FAYEL where they were billeted.	
	20		A very showery day. Training and Education classes resumed.	
	21		The whole Battalion were engaged in clearing up the roads in the village during the morning.	
	22		Church Parade on Battalion Parade Ground at 1100 hours.	
	23.		The Brigadier inspected the whole of the billets of the Battalion in MONTAGNE and LE FAYEL during the morning. The Drill was carried out from 09.30 hours to 1200 hours.	
	24		Education classes were held.	
	25		(Christmas Day) The day was observed as a holiday. Voluntary Church Parades were held in the morning for the Church of England and in the evening for Presbyterians.	
	26		Training from 0900 to 1300 hours. Neural Education classes. The last of the recruits left the Unit to return to their employment.	

A6945 Wt. W14422/M160 350,000 12/16 D. D. & L. Forms/C.2118/14.

Army Form C. 2118.

WAR DIARY
or
INTELLIGENCE SUMMARY.
(Erase heading not required.)

Place	Date	Hour	Summary of Events and Information	Remarks and references to Appendices
5/6th Scottish Rifles			December 1918	IX
	27	event	The Brigadier General inspected the transport of the Battalion in the main street of MONTAGNE at 10.30 hours and expressed himself satisfied with the turnout. The whole Battalion was bathed by Companies during the day at the Baths at CAMPS-EN-AMIENOIS	
	28.		The Battalion paraded at 09.30 hours for a Route March but owing to the unfavourable state of the weather this was cancelled and the companies returned to their billets.	
	29		Voluntary Divine Service held in the afternoon.	
	30 - 31		Training and Recreation was carried out as usual. On Hogmaney all officers of the Battalion had dinner together in a room of the MAIRIE at MONTAGNE. There was also a dinner for all Sergeants of the Battalion in MONTAGNE. Reinforcements received during the month:-	
			Lieut. A.B. White } 28 other ranks.	
			2/Lieut. E. Jowett }	

Army Form C. 2118.

WAR DIARY
or
INTELLIGENCE SUMMARY.
(Erase heading not required.)

Place	Date	Hour	Summary of Events and Information	Remarks and references to Appendices
576th Scottish Rifles			December 1918.	
			Strength of Battalion :-	
			Officers 35	
			Other Ranks 547	
			Hug W Spen	
			Lt Colonel	
			Commanding 576th Scottish Rifles	

Army Form C. 2118.

777/VU 51

52 O
8 sheets

WAR DIARY
or
INTELLIGENCE SUMMARY.
(Erase heading not required.)

5/6th Scottish Rifles   January 1919

Place	Date	Hour	Summary of Events and Information	Remarks and references to Appendices
MONTAGNE	1		New Year's Day was a holiday. All the Company held special Dinners which were visited by the Commanding Officer.	
	2		Training under Coy. arrangements in the morning at MONTAGNE and LE FAYEL. After dinner the G.O.C. 33rd Division presented medals to those of the Battn. who had not yet had them presented. This was done on parade and concluded with a march past in column of Companies.	
	3		Speech from the G.O.C. and a march past in column of Companies. The G.O.C. then inspected the troops.	
			Training carried on under Company arrangements. The morning Church Parade was also held.	
	4		Battalion Route March starting at MONTAGNE — WARLUS — ARRIGNE — ROAD — MONTAGNE. The one for Sunday.	
	5		Owing to weather and want of indoor accommodation no Church Parade could be held, but this was a voluntary service in the Sch____ DIENTRONE	
	6			

WAR DIARY or INTELLIGENCE SUMMARY

Army Form C. 2118.

Place	Date	Hour	Summary of Events and Information	Remarks and references to Appendices
Hd.Qr. Coy 2nd Rifles				
	6		Battalion employed clearing the village of MONTAGNE and getting bathed at CAMPS	
	7		Recognise training. Cleared up in billets owing to bad weather.	
	8		Route march ARAIGNE - MOULLENS VIDAME - CAMPS - ARAIGNE. In the evening a debate in the Recreation Room organised by the Education Officer. About 100 present.	
	9		Training under Coy arrangements. Lewis Gun Class fired on range at MONTAGNE.	
	10		Training under Coy arrangements. G.O.C. 33/Division visited MUNITIONS.	
	11		Coy training as usual. Also preparations for move to ROUEN.	
	12		Battalion moved by road to POIX via CAMPS and were billeted there for the night.	
	13		Battalion moved by train from POIX to ROUEN. Transport except cookers, one water cart and mess cart, going by road. Arrived Rouen at 5.30pm and marched to Reinforcement Camp. Headquarters details and "B" Coy at No. 1 Camp, "D" Coy at	

Army Form C. 2118.

WAR DIARY
or
INTELLIGENCE SUMMARY.
(Erase heading not required.)

January 1919

Place	Date	Hour	Summary of Events and Information	Remarks and references to Appendices
5/6th Bn Cameron Rifles				
			R.E. Camp. "A" Coy at Cavalry Camp and "B" Coy at No 2 Camp for Fatigue duty.	
	14		Company fatigue arrangements in the camps for accommodation etc.	
	15		Party made up to demobilization work at the Camps. Feb 19th	
			Infantry Brigade in command of all the Camps.	
	16/17		Training and Demobilization work under Coy arrangements. Various Camp fatigues	
	18		Company Officer left for leave in UK. Letter of thanks from the men supplied throughout the day. Provost of Hamilton.	I
			Asst Provost of Glasgow and from the Provost of Hamilton. Letter of Colonel opens for the June.	
			See Appendix I were received by Lt Colonel and presented to the City of Glasgow	
			Captured by the Battalion	
			and Borough of Hamilton	
	19		Church Parade in Y.M.C.A. Hut at 1100 hours followed by	
			Inspection of Camp and transport lines	
	20		Bks & Chair clothing for Battalion also novel fatigue duties	
	21		Accommodation officer inspected "B" Coy in F.M.O in Camp Brade	

WAR DIARY or INTELLIGENCE SUMMARY

Army Form C. 2118.

(4)

5th Bn Cameron Rifles   January 1919

Place	Date	Hour	Summary of Events and Information	Remarks and references to Appendices
			Guard and other Coy duties were under Coy arrangements. 4 officers attended an NCO's class conducting to N.W.	
	22		All but one Company employed on Guard duties over Camps & Prisoners. "C" Coy did Coy training	
	23		Guards, fatigues and football. Major C.C. Bell M.C. returned from leave and took over command.	
	24		Usual Guards & fatigues supplied by the Battalion.	
	25		Guards and fatigues same as for last two days. No men available for parade.	
	26		Brigade Church Parade in Y.M.C.A. Hut in No.2 Convalescent Camp. Battalion visited during the afternoon by G.O.C. 33rd Division. Guards as usual.	
	27		Guards and fatigues found by Battalion as before.	
	28		Guards and fatigues as usual.	
	29		Guards and fatigues as usual.	
	30		Guards and fatigues as usual. Lieut "A" Coy rejoined the Battalion from No.3 Dispersal Camp.	
	31			

Army Form C. 2118.

WAR DIARY
or
INTELLIGENCE SUMMARY.
(Erase heading not required.)

Instructions regarding War Diaries and Intelligence Summaries are contained in F. S. Regs., Part II. and the Staff Manual respectively. Title pages will be prepared in manuscript.

Place	Date	Hour	Summary of Events and Information	Remarks and references to Appendices
5/6th Bn. Scottish Rifles			January 1919	
	31		Battalion relieved of the No.58 General Hospital Guard by New Zealanders - Other Guards and fatigues as usual. — Strength of Battalion - 30 officers 491 other ranks	

Scott Major
Commg. 5/6th Scottish Rifles

5/6th Bn. Cameron Rifles

APPENDIX I

War Diary January 1919

war diary

City Chambers, Glasgow,

11th January, 1919.

Dear Colonel Spens,

    I have had the pleasure to receive your letter of 6th inst. intimating that you have instructed the War Trophies Committee to forward a Field Gun captured by your battalion on 9th October, 1918. I shall have great pleasure in receiving delivery of this historic memento of the war and the brilliant part taken in it by the Glasgow Battalion which you have the honour to command.

    With best wishes.

        I am,

            Yours very truly,

            [signature]

Lieut. Col. Hugh B. Spens, D.S.O.,
    Commanding 5/6th Batt. Scottish Rifles,
        B.E.F.,
           FRANCE.

WELL HALL,
HAMILTON.

TELEPHONE No. 172 HAMILTON.

war diary

13th January, 1919.

Dear Colonel Spens,

I duly received your letter of 6th inst., intimating that you have instructed the Trophies Committee at the War Office to forward to Hamilton one field gun captured by the Battalion.

I can assure you on behalf of the Town Council and the community that we shall very gladly accept this trophy, and find it a suitable position, as a permanent momento of the valour of the troops under your command. We have indeed been very anxious to get such a trophy and we appreciate very highly your thoughtfulness in having spontaneously remembered Hamilton in this connection.

With renewed thanks and Best Wishes,

I am,

Yours faithfully,

James Moffat.

PROVOST.

Lt. Col. Hugh B. Spens,
 Comdg., 5th/6th Bn., SCOTTISH RIFLES.

WAR DIARY
or
INTELLIGENCE SUMMARY.
(Erase heading not required.)

Army Form C. 2118.

Instructions regarding War Diaries and Intelligence Summaries are contained in F.S. Regs., Part II. and the Staff Manual respectively. Title pages will be prepared in manuscript.

5/6th Battalion SCOTTISH RIFLES.   Summary of Events and Information   FEBRUARY 1919.

Place	Date	Hour	Summary of Events and Information	Remarks and references to Appendices
Rouen	1/2/19		Battalion found the usual Guards and Fatigue duties.	
"	2/2/19		Usual Guards and Fatigues found. The Battalion attended the Brigade Presbyterian Church Service in the Y.M.C.A Hut No.2 Convalescent Camp at 10.30 hours.	
"	3/2/19		Town Picquet consisting of 2 officers and 20 other ranks at night found by the Battalion. Usual Guards and Fatigues found by the Battalion. Owing to an outbreak of Influenza in letter "A" Company the Company was moved to another hut and isolated from the rest of the Battalion for 3 days and struck off all duties. During the afternoon a Football Match was played between the Battalion and the 1st Cameronians on the Base Medical Board Depot ground. The Cameronians won by 2 goals to 1 goal.	
"	4/2/19		Usual Guards and Fatigues found by the Battalion.	
"	5/2/19		Usual Guards and Fatigues found by the Battalion. The Brigadier General inspected all the huts occupied by the Battalion at 10.00 hours also the Stores and Guardrooms.	
"	6-8/2/19		Usual Guards and Fatigues found by the Battalion.	
"	9/2/19		Battalion attended the Brigade Presbyterian Church Parade at 10.30 hours at the Y.M.C.A.Hut No.2 Convalescent Camp.	
"	10-15/2/19		Usual Guards and Fatigues found by the Battalion.	
"	16/2/19		Brigade Church Parade cancelled on account of rain.	
"	17/2/19		Usual Guards and Fatigues found by the Battalion.	
"	18/2/19		Usual Guards and Fatigues found by the Battalion. Draft of 8 Officers and 159 other ranks arrived from the 7th Scottish Rifles from Belgium.	
"	19/2/19		Usual Guards and Fatigues found by the Battalion. The new draft from the 7th Scottish Rifles inspected by the Brigadier General.	
"	20/2/19		Company parades held under Company arrangements from 09.15 to 12.00 hours.	
"	21/2/19		Companies paraded under Company arrangements between 09.15 to 12.00 hours handling of arms, Guard drill etc. The new Divisional General of the 33rd Division Major General Sir D.G.M.Campbell K.C.B. paid a visit to the Battalion during the morning.	

Army Form C. 2118.

WAR DIARY
or
INTELLIGENCE SUMMARY.
(Erase heading not required.)

Instructions regarding War Diaries and Intelligence Summaries are contained in F. S. Regs. Part II. and the Staff Manual respectively. Title pages will be prepared in manuscript.

Place	Date	Hour	Summary of Events and Information	Remarks and references to Appendices
			5/6th Battalion SCOTTISH RIFLES. FEBRUARY 1919.	
Rouen	22/2/19		Companies drilled under Company arrangements from 09.15 to 12.00 hours.	
"	23/2/19		The Battalion attended the Brigade Presbyterian Church Parade Service at 10.30 hours in the Y.M.C.A. Hut No.2 Convalescent Camp. After the service the Brigadier General took the salute of the Battalion when marching home.	
"	24/2/19		Companies drilled under Company arrangements from 09.15 to 12.00 hours.	
"	25/2/19		Companies drilled under Company arrangements from 09.15 to 12.00 hours. The Battalion found the firing party etc. for the funerals of two officers (Lieut.D.Prince R.N.R. and Lieut. Sikes 4th Hussars) at the Military Cemetery at Rouen at 14 hours.	
"	26/2/19		Companies drilled under Company arrangements from 09.15 hours to 12.05 hours.	
"	27/2/19		Companies drilled under Company arrangements from 09.15 to 12.15 hours. The Battalion found the firing party for the funeral of a V.A.D. at 14 hours at the Military Cemetery in Rouen.	
"	28/2/19		Companies drilled under Company arrangements from 09.15 hrs. until 12.15 hours. Usual Guards and Fatigues found by the Battalion. Strength of Battalion. Officers. 37 Other Ranks. 405 Reinforcements recieved during month. Lieut.S.LEOKIE. " T.L.MORRISON. " G.SHEARER. 2/Lt. G.BROOKS. " J.B.CLULOW. " F.CHRYSTAL. " F.HARVEY. " G&A.PEROTTI. " J.GILCHRIST. and 159 Other Ranks.	

Lieut. Colonel,
Commanding 5/6th Battalion Scottish Rifles.

Army Form C. 2118.

WAR DIARY
or
INTELLIGENCE SUMMARY.
(Erase heading not required.)

5/6th SCOTTISH RIFLES.   MARCH 1919.

Place	Date	Hour	Summary of Events and Information	Remarks and references to Appendices
Rouen.	Saturday 1st		The Battn. found the Firing Party for the funeral of Major E.T.Stanley. Labour Corps at the Military Cemetery ROUEN at 14.00 hours.	
"	Sunday 2nd		Summer time came into force at 23.00 hours. The Battn. attended the Brigade Presbyterian Church Parade at the Y.M.C.A. Hut at No.2 Con.Camp at 10.30 hours.	
"	Monday 3rd to) Saturday 8th)		The Battn. found the Guards for No. 58 General Hospitl.and the Field Punishment Compound as well as the ordinary Battn.Guard.	
"	Sunday 9th		The Battn. found the Guards for No. 58 General Hospital and the Field Punishment Compound. No Church Parade was held as all the men of the Battn. were bathed between 09.30 and 12.00 hours. The Commanding Officer inspected billets at 12.00 hours.	
"	Monday 10th		The Commanding Officer inspected the Battn. in full marching order on the Square at 10.00 hours after which the Battn. went for a short Route march.	
"	Tuesday 11th		The Commanding Officer inspected the Transport on the Square at 10.30 hours.	
"	Wednesday 12th		The Battn. was inspected in Marching Order on the square at 10.00 hours by Brigadier General C.G.R.Mayne. D.S.O. Commanding the 19th Infantry Brigade. The Battn. was drawn up in line and received the Brigadier with a General salute after which the Brigadier dismounted and made a minute inspection of the ranks. When this was completed the Brigadier called out all the Officers and addressed them and then the Battn. marched past in column of Route and proceeded for a Route March round the Camp Area.	
"	Thursday 13th		Company drill under Company Commanders from 09.30 to 12.00 hours.	
"	Friday 14th		No parades held during the morning owing to the rain. In the afternoon the Battn.played the 19th Field Ambulance at Football and beat them by 3 goals to 1.	
"	Saturday 15th		Companies drilled under Company arrangements from 09.30 to 12.00 hours. In the afternoon the Battn. played a team from the General Reinforcement Base Depot at Football result being a draw. The score 2 goals each.	
"	Sunday 16th		The Battn.attended the Brigade Presbyterian Church Parade at No. 2 Con. Camp at 11.00 hours. The Commanding Officer inspected billets at 12.00 hours. During the afternoon Guards for 58 General Hospl. and No. 5 W.A.A.C. Camp found by the Battn. Result Right Half Battn. 2 goals. Left Half Battn. 1 goal.	
"	Monday 17th		The Commanding Officer inspected the Right Half Battn. played the Left Half Battn. at Hockey. Result Right Half Guards for No. 58 General Hospl. and No.5 W.A.A.C. Camp found by the Battn. The Right Half Battn. allotted the Baths during the day.	

Army Form C. 2118.

WAR DIARY
or
INTELLIGENCE SUMMARY.

(Erase heading not required.)

5/6th SCOTTISH RIFLES.   MARCH 1919.

Instructions regarding War Diaries and Intelligence Summaries are contained in F.S. Regs., Part II. and the Staff Manual respectively. Title pages will be prepared in manuscript.

Place	Date	Hour	Summary of Events and Information	Remarks and references to Appendices
Rouen.	Tuesday 18th		The Left Half Battn. allotted the Baths in the morning. Guards for No. 58 General Hospl.and No. 5. W.A.A.C. Camp found by the Battn.	
"	Wednesday 19th		The Brigadier General Commanding 19th Infantry Brigade inspected the Transport Lines at 09.15 hours and the Battn.Camp at 09.45 hours. Guards for No. 58 General Hospl.and No. 5 W.A.A.C. Camp found by the Battn.	
"	Thursday 20th		Guards for No. 58 General Hospital and No. 5 W.A.A.C. Camp found by the Battn.	
"	Friday 21st)		" " " " " " " "	
"	Saturday 22nd)		" " " " " " " "	
"	Sunday 23rd.		The Battn.Attended the Brigade Presbyterian Church Parade at the Y.M.C.A. Hut No. 2 Con.Camp at 11.00 hours. Guards for No. 58 General Hospl. and No. 5 W.A.A.C. Camp found by the Battn.	
"	Monday. 24th.		The Commanding Officer inspected the huts at 12.00 hours. Very wet day so no parades held. The Battn.Found the Guards for No. 58 General Hospl. and No. 5 W.A.A.C. Camp.	
"	Tuesday 25th		Half the Battn. bathed at the baths. The other Half Battn bathed at the baths. Guards for No. 58 General Hospl.and No. 5 W.A.A.C. Camp found by the Battn.	
"	Wednesday. 26th.		Guards for No. 58 General Hospl. and No. 5 W.A.A.C. Camp found by the Battn.	
"	Thursday. 27th		6 Officers left the Battn. to join the 9th Battn. at Cologne. A draft of 9 Officers and 218 N.C.O's. and men arrived from the 18th Batt. Highland Light Infantry. to join the Battn.	
"	Friday 28th		The Commanding Officer inspected the new draft from the 18th H.L.I. at 10.00 hours. Guards for No. 58 General Hospl. and No. 5 W.A.A.C.Camp found by the Battn.	
"	Saturday 29th.		The G.O.C. 19th Inf. Bde. inspected the new draft of Officers and men from the 18th H.L.I. at 10.00 hours. Guards for No. 58 General Hospl. & No. 5 W.A.A.C. Camp found by the Battn.	
"	Sunday 30th.		The Battn.attended the Brigade Presbyterian Church Parade at the Y.M.C.A.Hut No. 2 Con.Camp at 11.00 hours. At the conclusion of the service the Battn.marched past the Brigadier General. The Commanding Officer inspected the huts on the return of the Battn.to Camp. Left Half Battn.	
"	Monday. 31st.		Guards for No. 58 General Hospl. & No. 5. W.A.A.C. Camp found by the Battn. Left Half Battn. allotted the baths during the morning. During the month a Billiard Handicap was held in the Sergeants Mess and this was won by C.Q.M.S. J. Gourlay.	

Army Form C. 2118.

WAR DIARY
or
INTELLIGENCE SUMMARY.
(Erase heading not required.)

5/6th SCOTTISH RIFLES.   MARCH 1919.

Instructions regarding War Diaries and Intelligence Summaries are contained in F. S. Regs., Part II. and the Staff Manual respectively. Title pages will be prepared in manuscript.

Place	Date	Hour	Summary of Events and Information	Remarks and references to Appendices
			Reinforcements received during month.	
			2/Lieut. L.D.WATSON. M.C. ⎫	
			Capt. L. DUNCAN. ⎪	
			Lieut. C.C. COWAN. ⎪	
			" T.B. WALKER. ⎬ from 18th Battn.	
			2/Lieut. R.A. SCOTT. ⎪ H.L.I.	
			" G. TAYLOR. ⎪	
			" G. BIRCHALL. ⎪	
			" F.M. GRONOUS. ⎭	
			" J. PARKIN.	
			" D.A. NICOLL	
			" R.C. SMITH	
			232 other ranks.	
			Strength of Battalion:	
			Officers 32	
			Other Ranks. 509	

-1 AVR 1919

[signature] Hugh B Spens
Lieut. Colonel,
Commanding 5/6th Battalion Scottish Rifles.

Army Form C. 2118.

WAR DIARY
or
INTELLIGENCE SUMMARY.

(Erase heading not required.)

5/6th Battn. SCOTTISH RIFLES.

Summary of Events and Information **APRIL 1919.**

Place	Date	Hour	Summary of Events and Information	Remarks and references to Appendices
ROUEN	1/4/19.		The Baths were allotted to the Battalion at 08.30 hours until 11.00 hours and "A" & "B" Coys. bathed.	
"	2/4/19		The Baths were allotted to the Battalion at 09.30 hours until 11.00 hours & H.Qrs."C"&"D"Coys.bathed. At 14.30 hours a Transport competition was held in a field near the Transport Lines. The judges were Lt-Col.Hyde Smith D.S.O. and Captain T.Macfie. M.C. of the Cameronians. The Prize Winners were HEAVY DRAFT HORSES (pairs) 1 Rfm. J.Bayston. 2 Driver G.Hall.A.S.C. 3 Rfm. R.Anderson. LIGHT DRAFT HORSES (pairs) 1 Rfm. C.Freeland. 2 Rfm.B.Murtie. 3 Rfm. H.McInally. PACK PONIES. 1 Rfm. J.B.McCall. BEST TURNED OUT OFFICERS CHARGERS. 1 Rfm. A.A.Richardson with "BOBBY" and "CHARLIE". 2 Rfm. Little with "BEAUTY" and "BUNTY".	
"	3/4/19.		The Audit Board assembled at 10.00 hours and audited the Battn.accounts for the quarter ending 1st April.	
"	4/4/19.		The Battn.Paraded at 09.45 hours as strong as possible and proceeded for a ROUTE MARCH in the vicinity of the Camp Area. In the afternoon the Battn.played a football match against a team from G.R.B.D. and won by 6 goals to nothing.	
"	5/4/19. 6/4/19.		Guards and Escorts furnished. The Battn.attended the Brigade Presbyterian Church Parade at the Y.M.C.A.Hut No.2 Con.Camp at 11 hours. The Battn.found the Guards for No.10 General Hospital.(British Prisoners Compound) and 58 General Hospital and No.5 Q.M.A.A.C. Camp. The Commanding Officer inspected the Huts occupied by the Battn. at 12.00 hours.	
"	7/4/19.		The Battn.Found the Guards for No.10 General Hospital.(German Prisoners Compound.)No.10 General Hospital (British Prisoners Compound). No.58 General Hospital and No.5 Q.M.A.A.C. Hostel. The Baths were allotted to "C" & "D" Coys. at 09.30 hours.	
"	8/4/19.		The Battn.found the Guards for No.10 General Hospital (German Prisoners Compound) No.10 General Hospital (British Prisoners Compound) No.58 General Hospital and No.5 Q.M.A.A.C. Hostel. The Baths were allotted to "A" & "B" Coys.at 08.30 hours. The O.C. 19th Infantry Brigade inspected the Huts occupied by the Battn. at 10 hours. The Commanding Officer inspected Letter "D" Coy. in Full Marching Order at 10.45 hours on the SQUARE.	
"	9/4/19.		The G.O.C.33rd Division paid a visit to the Battn. in the afternoon and inspected the Camp. The Battn.found the Guards for No.10 General Hospital(British Prisoners Compound) No.10 General Hospital(German Prisoners Compound) No.58 General Hospital and No.5 Q.M.A.A.C.Hostel. The Commanding Officer inspected Letter "A" Coy. on the Square in Full Marching Order at 10.30 hours.	

Army Form C. 2118.

WAR DIARY
or
INTELLIGENCE SUMMARY.

(Erase heading not required.)

Place	Date	Hour	Summary of Events and Information	Remarks and references to Appendices
ROUEN	10/4/19. to 12/4/19.		5/6th Battn. SCOTTISH RIFLES. APRIL 1919. The Battn.found the Guards for No.10 General Hospital (German Prisoners Compound) No.10 General Hospital (British Prisoners Compound) No.58 General Hospital and No.5 Q.M.A.A.C.Hostel.	
"	13/4/19.		Guards found for No.10 General Hospital(German Prisoners Compound) No.10 General Hospital (British Prisoners Compound) No. 58 General Hospital and No.5 Q.M.A.A.C.Hostel. The Battn.attended the Brigade Presbyterian Church Parade at the Y.M.C.A.Hut No.2 Con.Camp at 11 hours. A party of N.C.O's. and Men representing the Battn.attended the Ceremony of placing wreaths on the graves of members of the Navy s and Armies of the Allied Nations as arranged by "Le Comité Du Souvenir Français" at the St.Sever Cemetery at Rouen at 10 hours. The Commanding Officer inspected the huts occupied by the Battn.at 12.00 hours.	
"	14/4/19.) to 17/4/19.)		The Battn. found the Guards for No.10 General Hospital(German Prisoners Compound) No.10 General Hospital(British Prisoners Compound) No. 58 General Hospital and No.5 Q.M.A.A.C. Hostel.	
"	18/4/19.		Guards found as yesterday. The Battn.played a team from the 10th Scottish Rifles at Football in the afternoon and were beaten. Scores: 10th Scottish Rifles 4 goals. 5/6th Scottish Rifles Nil.	
"	19/4/19.		Guards as before. The Battn.attended the Brigade Presbyterian Service at the Y.M.C.A.Hut No. 2 Con.Camp at 11 hours.	
"	20/4/19.		Guards as before. The Commanding Officer inspected the huts occupied by the Battn. at 12 hours. The Battn.in conjunction with the 39th Divisional H.Qrs. and the 19th Field Ambulance held a Sports Meeting in the afternoon on the Battn.ground. The results were. 100 Yards Flat Race. 220 yards Flat Race. 1. R.S.M. Cox. 39th Divisional H.Qrs. 1. R.S.M.Cox. 39th Divisional H.Qrs. 2. Pte. Hunter. 19th Field Ambulance. 2. Pte.Hunter 19th Field Ambulance. 3. Cpl. Elias. 5/6th Sco.Rifles. 3. Cpl.Elias. 5/6th Sco.Rifles 440 yards Flat Race. V.A.D. Egg & Spoon Race. 1. Pte.Hunter. 19th Field Ambulance. 1.Pte.Atkinson 19th Fld.Amb. 1. Miss Hart. 2. Rfm.Henderson 5/6th Sco.Rifles. 2 Rfm.Paton 5/6thSco.Rifles 2. Miss Jack. 3.Cpl.Elias " 3. Miss Ackland. High Jump. Long Jump. Boot Race. 1.Rfm.Fleming 5/6th Sco.Rifs. 1 Pte.Jardine. 5/6th Sco.Rifs. 1. Pte.Atkinson 19th Fd.Amb. 2.Rfm.Henderson " 2 Rfm.Henderson " 2.Rfm.Campbell.5/6th Sco.Rifs. 3.Rfm.Smith. " ride & Drive Competition. Wrestling on Horseback. Horse Jumping Officers. 1.39th Div.H.Qrs.Team. 1.19th Field Amb.Team. 1.Lieut.Grant.10thSco.Rifs. 2.19th Field Amb. 2.5/6th Sco.Rifles " 2. " Burden.5/6th Sco.Rifs. Horse Jumping W.Os. N.C.O's. & Men. 1st. B.S.M. Allovers R.F.A. 2nd. B.S.M Robinson. R.F.A.	

(3).

Army Form C. 2118.

WAR DIARY
or
INTELLIGENCE SUMMARY.

(Erase heading not required.)

Instructions regarding War Diaries and Intelligence Summaries are contained in F. S. Regs., Part II. and the Staff Manual respectively. Title pages will be prepared in manuscript.

Place	Date	Hour	Summary of Events and Information	Remarks and references to Appendices
			5/6th Battn. SCOTTISH RIFLES. APRIL 1919.	
ROUEN.	21/30/4/19		Guards and Escorts furnished daily.	
			Strength of Battalion.	
			Officers................28	
			Other ranks.............551	
			Reinforcements received. 46	
			J. L. Maclachlan	
			Captain	
			Commanding 5/6th Battn. Scottish Rifles.	

Army Form C. 2118.

5/6 Scottish Rifles

560
2 sheet

WAR DIARY
or
INTELLIGENCE SUMMARY.
(Erase heading not required.)

Instructions regarding War Diaries and Intelligence Summaries are contained in F. S. Regs., Part II. and the Staff Manual respectively. Title pages will be prepared in manuscript.

Place	Date	Hour	Summary of Events and Information	Remarks and references to Appendices
Rouen.	1/5/19.		5/6th Batt. SCOTTISH RIFLES.	
"	2/5/19.		Battalion Training. Drill Lewis Gun practice P.T. & B.F. etc.	
			Battalion inspected by Brigadier General L.F.Phillips. C.M.G. C.B.E. D.S.O. Base Commandant.	
			He wished all ranks to know he was very pleased with the state of the Battn.in every respect.	
"	3/5/19.		Training.	
"	4/5/19.		The Battn.furnished guards as under:-	
			No. 25 Stationary Hospl. 11 O.Rs. Launay Petrol Guard 14 O.Rs.	
			Quarter Guard. 8 O.Rs. No.6 Genl.Hospl. 11 O.Rs.	
			Safe Custody Compound. 14 O.Rs. No.5 Q.M.A.A.C.Hostel. 4 O.Rs.	
			No.10 Genl.Hospl.(G.P.C.)26 O.Rs.	
			Total 88 O.Rs.	
			Remainder of Battn. attended Church Parades.	
"	5/9th/5/19.		Guards found for No. 25 Stationary Hospl. Launay Petrol Dump. The Safe Custody Compound.	
			No. 10 Genl.Hospl. No. 6 Genl.Hospl and No. 5 Q.M.A.A.C.Hostel.	
"	10/5/19.		Companies trained under Company Commanders.	
"	11/5/19.		The Batt.attended The Brigade Presbyterian Service at 11.00 hours at the Y.M.C.A. Hut in the	
			Medical Board Base Depot. The Commanding Officer inspected the mens Huts at 12.00 hours.	
"	12/5/19.)		Companies trained under Company arrangements from 09.00 to 12.00 hours daily.	
	13/5/19.)		R.S.M's. Class for Junior N.C.O's at 12.00 hours daily each day.	
	14/5/19.		The Commanding Officer inspected Letter "B" Coy. at 09.30 hours and letter "C" Coy. at 11.30 hours.	
			in full Marching Order on the Square.	
			At 20.00 hours the Concert Party of No. 2 Despatch Camp gave a special GALA Performance to all	
			ranks of the Battn. in the Theatre in No. 2 Despatch Camp.	
"	15/5/19/17/5/19.		Companies trained under Company arrangements from 09.00 to 12.00 hours daily. Lewis Gun	
			Classes held and R.S.M's. Class.	
"	18/5/19.		Battn.attended the Brigade Presbyterian Service at the Y.M.C.A. Hut. Medical Board Base Depot at	
			11.00 hours. The Commanding Officer inspected the Huts occupied by the Battn. at 12.00 hours.	
"	19/5/19/24/5/19.		The Battn. found the following guards daily.(B.P.C.) Vehicle Park Rive Gauche Station.	
			No.10 Genl.Hospl.(G.P.C.) No. 10 Genl.Hospl.(B.P.C.) Field Punishment Compound.	
			No.5 Q.M.A.A.C. Camp. Field Punishment Compound.	
			Junior Officers Classes held daily.	
"	25/5/19.		The Battn.attended the Brigade Presbyterian Church Service Parade at the Y.M.C.A.Hut Medical Board	
			Base Depot at 11.00 hours. The Commanding Officer inspected all the Huts occupied by the	
			Battn. at 12.00 hours.	

Army Form C. 2118.

WAR DIARY
or
INTELLIGENCE SUMMARY.

(Erase heading not required.)

(2).

Instructions regarding War Diaries and Intelligence Summaries are contained in F.S. Regs., Part II. and the Staff Manual respectively. Title pages will be prepared in manuscript.

Place	Date	Hour	Summary of Events and Information	Remarks and references to Appendices
Rouen.	26/5/19.		5/6th Battn. Scottish Rifles.	
			Guards found for Vehicle Park Rive Gauche Station. Field Punishment Compound. No.6 Genl. Hospl. and No.5 Q.M.A.A.C. Camp.	
			The Advance Party of the Battn. for CALAIS left the GARE Du NORD at 16.30 hours.	
			Junior Officers Class Held.	
"	27/31/5/19.		Guards found for the Vehicle Park Rive Gauche Station. F.P. Compound. No.6 Genl. Hospl and No.5 Q.M.A.A.C. Camp.	
			Junior Officers Class held daily.	
			Strength of the Battalion 31/5/19.	
			Officers 36	
			O.Rs. 519	
			Officers joined during the month	
			2/Lieut. Fyfe R.R. 2/2 Sco.Horse. 2/Lieut. Burnett S.E.S. 2/2.Sco.Horse.	
			2/Lieut. Evans J.J.7/Sherwood Foresters. 2/Lieut. Key A.E. 2/1 Fife & Forfar Yeomanry.	
			2/Lieut. Kidd E.G.L. 2/2 Sco. Horse.	
			All the above transferred from 1/4 R.S.F. with effect from 4/5/19.	
			Lieut. Berry Hart R.A. 8/Seaforths 2/Lieut. Hart W.D. 3/Seaforths.	
			" Hamilton J. do " Hall D.H. Seaforths.	
			" Hawthorne R.H. do " Montgomery W.M. "	
			All the above transferred 9th Seaforths (S) Pioneers 3/5/19.	
			Officers left during month: 2/Lieut. Hardie G. to U.K. for dispersal 22/5/19.	
			2/Lieut. Parkin J. " " "	

(signed) Cb Scott Major

Commanding 5/6th Battalion Scottish Rifles.

CONFIDENTIAL

Army Form C. 2118.

5/6 Scottish Rifles

57 Sheet

WAR DIARY
INTELLIGENCE SUMMARY
(Erase heading not required.)

Instructions regarding War Diaries and Intelligence Summaries are contained in F. S. Regs., Part II. and the Staff Manual respectively. Title pages will be prepared in manuscript.

Place	Date	Hour	Summary of Events and Information	Remarks and references to Appendices
ROUEN.	SUNDAY 1st Jun 1919.		Found Guards for :— Whistle Post, RIVE GAUCHE Stn Field President Compound. No 6 General Hospital. No 5 Q.M.A.A.C. Camp. Battalion attended at Divine Service in Y.M.C.A. hut, Medical Board Room Dpt at 11.00 hrs. Commanding Officer inspected huts and institutes etc at 12.00 hrs. 19th Infantry Brigade Sports were held at the ROUEN FOOTBALL CLUB GROUND at 14.30 hrs. Events won by the Battalion were :— DISPATCH RACE. 3 Prizes in OBSTACLE RACE. 3rd Prize in HIGH JUMP (Cpl T. MORRISON)	
"	MONDAY 2nd Jun 1919.		Usual P.O.W. Escort found. Training under Coy arrangements. Cymbals under Signalling Officer. R.S.M's Parade for N.C.O's at 12.00 hrs.	
"	TUESDAY 3rd Jun 1919.		Usual P.O.W. Escort found. Training under Company arrangements. Cymbals under Signalling Officer. R.S.M's Parade for N.C.O's at 12.00 hrs.	

CONFIDENTIAL

Army Form C. 2118.

WAR DIARY
or
INTELLIGENCE SUMMARY.
(Erase heading not required.)

Instructions regarding War Diaries and Intelligence Summaries are contained in F. S. Regs., Part II. and the Staff Manual respectively. Title pages will be prepared in manuscript.

Place	Date	Hour	Summary of Events and Information	Remarks and references to Appendices
ROUEN.	WEDNESDAY 4th June 1919.		Usual P.O.W. Escort founds. Training under Company arrangements. Signalled under Signalling Officer. R.S.M'S Class for N.C.O's.	
"	THURSDAY 5th June 1919.		Usual P.O.W. Escort founds. Training under Company arrangements. Signalled under Signalling Officer. R.S.M'S Class for N.C.O's.	
"	FRIDAY 6th June 1919		Usual P.O.W. Escort founds. Training under Company arrangements. Signalled under Signalling Officer. R.S.M'S Class for N.C.O's.	
"	SATURDAY 7th June 1919.		Usual P.O.W. Escort and usual training.	
"	SUNDAY 8th June 1919.		Battalion attended at Divine Service in Y.M.C.A. Hut. Medical Board Sptd at 11.00 hrs. Connecting Officer inspected huts at institutes at at 12.00 hrs.	

CONFIDENTIAL

Army Form C. 2118.

WAR DIARY
or
INTELLIGENCE SUMMARY.
(Erase heading not required.)

Instructions regarding War Diaries and Intelligence Summaries are contained in F. S. Regs., Part II. and the Staff Manual respectively. Title pages will be prepared in manuscript.

Place	Date	Hour	Summary of Events and Information	Remarks and references to Appendices
ROUEN.	MONDAY. 9th June 1919.		Whitsuntide - a holiday.	
"	TUESDAY. 10th June 1919.		Usual P.O.W. Escort and usual training. The Commanding Officer inspected "A" & "D" Coys in Full Marching Order.	
"	WEDNESDAY. 11th June 1919.		Usual P.O.W. Escort and usual training. The Officer Commanding 19th Infty Brigade inspected the Battalion (including Transport) at 10.00 hrs. DRESS: Marching Order. FORMATION: Battalion in LINE.	
"	THURSDAY. 12th June 1919.		Usual P.O.W. Escort. Found Guards for: No 2 Military Prison. No 10 Labour Camp. 41st Dutch Labour Coy. The Commanding Officer inspected "B" & "C" Coys in Full Marching Order.	
"	FRIDAY. 13th June 1919.		Usual P.O.W. Escort. The Commanding Officer inspected all "Regimental Empty" in Full Marching Order.	
"	SATURDAY. 14th June 1919.		Usual P.O.W. Escort. Training over Barrack Square 9.30 a.m. to 11. Suffolk Regt. Party of Officers for move to CALAIS. 5 Lorry loads of Stores dumped at night at GARE DU NORD and guards.	

CONFIDENTIAL

Army Form C. 2118.

WAR DIARY

~~INTELLIGENCE SUMMARY~~

(Erase heading not required.)

Instructions regarding War Diaries and Intelligence Summaries are contained in F.S. Regs., Part II. and the Staff Manual respectively. Title pages will be prepared in manuscript.

Place	Date	Hour	Summary of Events and Information	Remarks and references to Appendices
ROUEN	SUNDAY 15th Jan 1919		Page First. Transport moved off at 04.30 hrs for GARE BUNOD and moved with 1st TRAIN TO CALAIS. Loading of train completed by 10 a.m. Bn. marched to GARE DU NORD by road:— N°2 DESPATCH CAMP — RUE DELBEIF — RUE LAFAYETTE — PONT CORNEILLE — QUAI DE PARIS — BOULEVARD GAMBETTA — GARE DUNORD. Entrained for CALAIS at 16.00 hrs. Travelling to CALAIS all afternoon and night. Baggage 1st B. Telemometerhaupter Montatote	
CALAIS	MONDAY 16th Jan 1919		Bn. arrived in CALAIS about 10.30 hrs at SAND DUNES Sth. Marched to ETON CAMP, BEADMARSHS — Canvas camp.	
"	TUESDAY 17th Jan 1919		Quarter Guard and Fire Piquet for B. only formed. Cleaning of camp which was not too clean.	
"	WEDNESDAY 18th Jan 1919		P.O.W. Escorts found for No.15 P.O.W. Coy. and No.76 P.O.W. Coy. Training under Company Arrangements. 6 N.C.Os sent to 37th Divisional School.	
"	THURSDAY 19th Jan 1919		Usual P.O.W. Escorts out. Training under Company Arrangements.	
"	FRIDAY 20th Jan 1919		Usual P.O.W. Escorts out. Training under Company Arrangements.	

WAR DIARY
INTELLIGENCE SUMMARY
(Erase heading not required)

Army Form C. 2118.

Place	Date	Hour	Summary of Events and Information (see over)	Remarks and references to Appendices
CALAIS.	SATURDAY. 21st June 1919.		Usual P.O.W. Escorts and a Piquet to patrol CANAL DU MARCK to prevent bathing. Training under Company Arrangements.	
"	SUNDAY. 22nd June 1919.		Burial the March piquet funds. 1 Officer, 1 W.O. & 3 Sgts. proceed on excursion to OSTEND. Battalion attended Divine Service in Y.M.C.A. Hut in HARROW CAMP at 09.30 hrs.	
"	MONDAY. 23rd June 1919.		Usual P.O.W. Escorts and Canal du Marck Piquet funds. Training under Company Arrangements.	
"	TUESDAY. 24th June 1919.		No.125 P.O.W. Coy Escorts only, and Canal du Marck piquet funds. 3 Offrs. proc. to School of Cookery, AUBENGUE for instruction. Training under Company Arrangements. Batty. Parade at O.N. Bivouac for "B", "C", "D" Coys and H.Q.	
"	WEDNESDAY. 25th June 1919.		No.125 P.O.W. Coy and G.B.D. Escorts and Canal du Marck piquet funds. Training under Company Arrangements. Batty. Parade at O.N. Bivouac for "A" Cy.	
"	THURSDAY. 26th June 1919.		Usual P.O.W. Escorts and Canal du Marck piquet funds. Route March from 08.00 hrs to 12.00 hrs - along Sands.	

WAR DIARY
INTELLIGENCE SUMMARY

CONFIDENTIAL
Army Form C. 2118.

Instructions regarding War Diaries and Intelligence Summaries are contained in F.S. Regs., Part II. and the Staff Manual respectively. Title pages will be prepared in manuscript.

(Erase heading not required.)

Summary of Events and Information

Page Six

Place	Date	Hour	Summary of Events and Information	Remarks and references to Appendices
CALAIS.	FRIDAY. 27th June 1919.		Usual P.O.W. Escorts. Training under Company arrangements.	
"	SATURDAY. 28th June 1919.		Usual P.O.W. Escorts. Training under Company Arrangements. Ladies five other ranks attended CALAIS BASE Horse Show at LES BARAQUES.	
"	SUNDAY. 29th June 1919.		Battalion attended Divine Service in Y.M.C.A. Hut HACKNEY CAMP at 10.30 hours. 4 Officers and 20 other ranks attended 35th DIVISIONAL RACE MEETING at BOULOGNE. Battalion found a party of 4 Officers and 100 other ranks for fire fighting at fire in ORDNANCE DUMP, BEAUMARAIS at also a fighting party of 1 Officer and 20 other ranks from 20.00 hours till 10.00 hours 30th June 1919.	
"	MONDAY. 30th June 1919.		Escorts found for No. 125 and 77 P.O.W. Coys and G.B.D. Training under Company arrangements - 6 Reinforcements from East Coy under training carried by Battalion.	

Strength at 30th June 1919.
34. Officers. 494. Other Ranks.

WAR DIARY
INTELLIGENCE SUMMARY
(Erase heading not required.)

Army Form C. 2118.

CONFIDENTIAL

Instructions regarding War Diaries and Intelligence Summaries are contained in F.S. Regs., Part II. and the Staff Manual respectively. Title pages will be prepared in manuscript.

Place	Date	Hour	Summary of Events and Information	Remarks and references to Appendices
			Page Sixteen	
			Officers who had joined the Battalion during June 1919.	
			Captain A.C. STEWART. M.C. from Sick Leave in U.K. 1/6/19.	
			Captain W.H. HUTCHISON. O.T attached from 20/6/19.	
			Officers who had quitted the Battalion during June 1919.	
			Captain J. CLARK. M.C., M.M. to U.K. for Dispersal 5/6/19.	
			Captain D.N. MACLACHLAN. M.C. Posted to 9th Bn. Scottish Rifles as Adjutant 3/6/19.	
			2/Lieut. G. BROOKS. M.M. to Hospital sick 21/6/19.	
			<u>Honours and Awards.</u> (Extracts from London Gazette of 3/6/19.)	
			Captain (temp. Lieut-Col.) H.B. SPENS. D.S.O. to be Brevet Major.	
			200146 R.Q.M.S. J. McK. GOURLAY awarded M.S.M.	
			200149 Sergeant W. McGHIE awarded M.S.M.	
			200629 R.S.M. P. DOCHERTY. M.M. awarded D.C.M.	
			201248 C.S.M. R. FORSYTH awarded D.C.M.	

Scott Major
Commanding 5/6th Battn. SCOTTISH RIFLES

5/6 Scottish Rifles
Vol 57

WAR DIARY
INTELLIGENCE SUMMARY.

Place	Date	Hour	Summary of Events and Information	Remarks and references to Appendices
Calais	TUESDAY 1/7/19		Battalion furnished P. of W. escorts to Q.B.A. 135 and No 97 P.of W. Coy. Company training under Company Commanders. Signallers training under Signalling Officer. Lewis Gun Classes under Lewis Gun N.C.O.	
	WEDNESDAY 2/7/19		Battn furnished P.of W. escorts to Q.B.A. No 125 and 16 yy P. of W. Coy. Company training under Company Commanders. Signallers trained under Signalling Officer. Lewis Gun Classes under Lewis Gun N.C.O. The Area Commandant (Colonel Colchester Wemyss) inspected the Camp and said that Great progress had been made and cleanliness and order since the Battalion took over.	
	THURSDAY 3/7/19		Battn furnished P.of W. escorts to Q.B.A. No 125 and No 97 P. of W. Coy. Coy training under Coy Commanders. Signallers trained under Signalling Officer. Lewis Gun Classes under Lewis Gun N.C.O. Battn Audit Board on Regimental Accounts assembled.	
	FRIDAY 4/7/19		Battn furnished P. of W. escorts to Q.B.A., No 125 and No 97 P. of W. Coy.	

Army Form C. 2118.

WAR DIARY
or
INTELLIGENCE SUMMARY.
(Erase heading not required.)

Summary of Events and Information

Page 11

Place	Date	Hour	Summary of Events and Information	Remarks and references to Appendices
Calais	FRIDAY 4/7/19		A, B + C Coys. trained under Coy. Commanders on Coy. Parade Ground. Battalion played 10th Batt. Scottish Rifles at football on Aerodrome Ground, the game ending in a draw of 4 goals each.	
	SATURDAY 5/7/19		Battalion training consisted of a route march of all available ranks to the village of Marck and back. The distance covered was approximately ten miles. The Brigade Commander took the salute as the Battalion returned to camp.	
	SUNDAY 6/7/19		The Divisional (59th) Church Parade and Thanksgiving Service for Victory Peace was held on the Aerodrome Ground, Calais at 10.00 hours. At the conclusion the Pipe Band of the Battalion played the march past of nearly 3,000 Troops. A party of Officers N.C.O.'s and men proceeded on an excursion to the Battlefield and Mont des Cats Areas.	
	MONDAY 7/7/19		Battn. provided escorts to L.B.A., No 125 and No 4 Pot. W Coys. Coys. trained under Coy. Commanders. In the afternoon the Battn. trained in musketry on Calais Rifle Range. Tea was served on the Range. Practices 1, 2 and 3 were fired.	

Army Form C. 2118.

WAR DIARY
INTELLIGENCE SUMMARY.
(Erase heading not required.)

Instructions regarding War Diaries and Intelligence Summaries are contained in F. S. Regs., Part II. and the Staff Manual respectively. Title pages will be prepared in manuscript.

Page 3.

Place	Date	Hour	Summary of Events and Information	Remarks and references to Appendices
Calais	TUESDAY 8/7/19		Battn furnished escorts to R.B.A. No 125 and 74 P of W. Corps. Baths were allotted to A + B Coys.	
	WEDNESDAY 9/7/19		Battn furnished escorts to R.B.A. No 125 and 74 P of W. Corps. Baths were allotted to B Coy.	
	THURSDAY 10/7/19		Battn furnished escorts to R.B.A. No 125 and 74 P of W. Corps. Garrison duties were found for No 2 Labour Group of No 1 Main Guard, No 2 Main Guard and No 3 Main Guard, and Calais Dunes Station Guard. (208 i.e. 2 Sergts. 4 Corporals & 45 men).	
	FRIDAY 11/7/19		Battn furnished escorts to No 125 & 74 P of W Corps. Garrison duties were found for No 2 Labour Group of No 1, 2, & 3 Main Guards and Calais Dunes Station Guard.	
	SATURDAY 12/7/19		Battn furnished escorts to R.B.A. No 125 & 74 P of W Corps. Guards found were:- No 1 Main Guard No 2 Main Guard No 3 Main Guard Calais Dunes Station Guard. A rehersal was held of the part to be taken by a Company of 5 Officers and 150 men of the Battn. in the French Peace celebrations in Calais	

Army Form C. 2118.

WAR DIARY
INTELLIGENCE SUMMARY.
(Erase heading not required.)

Instructions regarding War Diaries and Intelligence Summaries are contained in F. S. Regs., Part II. and the Staff Manual respectively. Title pages will be prepared in manuscript.

Place	Date	Hour	Summary of Events and Information	Remarks and references to Appendices
Calais	SUNDAY 13/7/19		Page 4 Battn attended Church Parade, for the various denominations, in camp. Nos 1, 2 & 3 man guards, Calais Junct. Station Guard, were furnished at No 2 Labour Group.	
	MONDAY 14/7/19		Guards were furnished for Nos 1, 2, & 3 man guards of No 2 Labour Group and Calais Junct. Station. A Company of 5 officers and 100 other ranks from the Battalion took part in the French Peace Celebrations and a march past the officer governing the town of Calais (General Ditte). At the conclusion the boy was congratulated on its appearance and the following congratulatory orders were subsequently received Congratulatory order "From Base Commandant, Calais To O.C. Troops, Beaumarais "I wish to congratulate the company of the 5/6th Scottish Rifles on its excellent drill at the review yesterday. The march past was extraordinarily good and the general appearance and	

WAR DIARY

INTELLIGENCE SUMMARY.

(Erase heading not required.)

Army Form C. 2118.

Page 5

Place	Date	Hour	Summary of Events and Information	Remarks and references to Appendices
Calais	MONDAY 14/7/19		"All of the men worthily maintained the prestige of the British Army, and of the distinguished Regiment to which they belong." (Signed) W. D. Logan, Brig. General. Base Commandant, Calais.	
	TUESDAY 15/7/19		Escorts found for GBD and No 125 PofW. boy. Guards were furnished for Nos 1, 2, & 3 Main Guards at No 2 Labour Group and Calais Dunes Station Guard. Baths were allotted to AVB boys.	
	WEDNESDAY 16/7/19		Escorts were found for GBD and No 125 PofW boy. Guards were furnished for No 1, 2 & 3 Main Guards at No 2 Labour Group and Calais Dunes Station. Lewis Run Class fired on Calais Dunes Rifle Range in the afternoon.	
	THURSDAY 17/7/19		Guards were furnished for No 1, 2, 3 Main Guards at No 2 Labour Group Calais Dunes Station. Escorts found for GBD, and No 125 PofW Coys.	
	FRIDAY 18/7/19		Calais Dunes Station. Guards found for No 1, 2, 3 Main Guards at No 2 Labour Group Calais Dunes Station. The Commanding Officer inspected the	

WAR DIARY
or
INTELLIGENCE SUMMARY

Army Form C. 2118.

Place	Date	Hour	Summary of Events and Information	Remarks and references to Appendices
Calais	FRIDAY 18/4/19		Page 2 employed men of the Batt. at 14.15 hours Brigadier General B.J. Price C.B., C.M.G., D.S.O. assumed command of 19th Infantry Brigade.	
	16/4/19		Escorts were found for No. 125 P.O.W. Coy r C.B.D. Brig. Genl. B.J. Price C.B., C.M.G., D.S.O. inspected the Camp at 09.30 hours.	
	SATURDAY 19/4/19		Guards were found for No. 1, 2, r 3. Main Guards at No. 2 Labour Group and Calais Aunée Station.	
	SUNDAY 20/4/19		Guards found for No. 1, 2, r 3. Main Guards at No. 2 Labour Group. Church Parades for the various denominations were held in the Camp Area. 1 Officer and 7 other ranks proceeded on an excursion to Ypres. 2 Officers r 30 other ranks proceeded on an excursion to Bailleul.	
	MONDAY 21/4/19		Guards were found for No. 1, 2, r 3. Main Guards at No. 2 Labour Group. Escorts were found for C.B.D. and No. 125 P.O.W. Coy. Battn. Arms Coy Luis been assembled. Batt. Bland r Cooper, Battn. Arms were allotted to B.r D. Coys. Major Genl. E.S. Bulfin Transfer at 10.00 hours. C.Ron C.Rogers Lt. Col Lt. Col Commanding 2nd. Bn. Royal Welsh Fusiliers	

WAR DIARY

INTELLIGENCE SUMMARY.

Army Form C. 2118.

Page 4

Place	Date	Hour	Summary of Events and Information	Remarks and references to Appendices
Calais	TUESDAY 22/1/19		Guards were furnished to Nos. 1, 2 & 3 Main Guard. at No 2 Labour Group. Scouts were found for G.B.D. & No 125 P of W Corp. Baths were allotted to B.A. Corp & Bath N Gp=	
	WEDNESDAY 23/1/19		Usual guards & P of W Scouts found by the Battalion. Battalion messing committee was formed.	
	THURSDAY 24/1/19		Usual guards & P of W Scouts found. Corps nor finding guards. Issued under Corp Commanders. Ribbon for British War medal 1914-1919 was issued	
	FRIDAY 25/1/19		Usual Guards & P of W Scouts found.	
	SATURDAY 26/1/19		Usual Guards & P of W Scouts found.	
	SUNDAY 27/1/19		Do	
	MONDAY 28/1/19		Church parade for various denominations was held in Camp. Usual Guards & P of W Scouts found. Baths allotted to C.P. Corp &	
	TUESDAY 29/1/19		Do	
	WEDNESDAY 30/1/19		Do Baths allotted to B Group	

WAR DIARY
INTELLIGENCE SUMMARY.
(Erase heading not required.)

Army Form C. 2118.

Page 8.

Place	Date	Hour	Summary of Events and Information	Remarks and references to Appendices
Calais	Thursday 31/7/19		Hour Guards & 5th W. Scott to found. Strength at 31/7/19 Officers — 24 Other Ranks — 1115 Officers joined during the month. Captain Wilburne W. Chaplain joined 11/7/19 Officers quitted during the month. Lieut A.R. Kay 2/1 Life & Forfar Yeomanry — to Calais as Embarcation Officer 1/7/19 Lieut Col N.B. Gow DSO 5 Scottish Rifles — to demobilization 11/7/19 2/Lt J.N. Groones 4th N.F.] 23/7/19 Lieut G.C. Dowan 14th R.F.] to 119th N.F. 22/7/19 Lieut J.B. Walker MC 5 N.F.] to 119th N.F. 28/7/19 Capt W.H. Hutcheson Chaplain to demobilization 11/7/19 Calais 1/8/19 [signature] C.P. Scott Lewis B. Jones Comdg 5/6 H.B. Scottish Rifles	

5/6 Scott Rifles

Army Form C. 2118.

WAR DIARY
— of —
INTELLIGENCE SUMMARY.
(Erase heading not required.)

Instructions regarding War Diaries and Intelligence Summaries are contained in F. S. Regs., Par. II. and the Staff Manual respectively. Title pages will be prepared in manuscript.

Place	Date	Hour	Summary of Events and Information	Remarks and references to Appendices
Calais	1/5/19		Duties as usual. At 17:00 hours 29th Br. temp. Leaved Regmt took on from 40th the following duties. No 1, 2, + 3 Main Guards, Silver Dome Stn. Guard at No 2 Labour Guard.	59 3 sheets
"	2/5/19		Took on following guards from 25th K.R.R. (1) 1st Brigade H.Q. (2) Infantry Stn. (3) Vehicle Park. (4) No 6 Ordnance Depôt (night guard only).	
"	3/5/19		Duties as usual. Church Parades of all denominations. No 3978 Cpl Davidson when bathing with R.C. made, was accidentally drowned.	
"	4/5/19		Duties as usual. Empire Bank Holiday was called a holiday.	
"	5/5/19		Duties as usual. Conference at Brigade H.Q. re changing of guards.	
"	6/5/19		Duties as usual.	
"	7/5/19		do Warlingeroge Cup started in B Co.	
"	8/5/19		do E. Coy did musketry in range result good.	
"	9/5/19		do	
"	10/5/19		do Church Parade for all denominations	
"	11/5/19		do Brigade Patrol at 19:30 hours to search for escaped O.B.W. 18 Officer 86R	
"	12/5/19		do Inspected Camp of S.6.C. 59 Div. Coy who informed himself well satisfied with the cleanliness of the camp.	

WAR DIARY
or
INTELLIGENCE SUMMARY.
(Erase heading not required.)

Army Form C. 2118.

Instructions regarding War Diaries and Intelligence Summaries are contained in F.S. Regs., Part II. and the Staff Manual respectively. Title pages will be prepared in manuscript.

Place	Date	Hour	Summary of Events and Information	Remarks and references to Appendices
Calais	13/5/19		Duties as usual. B⁻ held in camp.	
	14/5/19		Inspection of transport by G.O.C. 9th Bgde. who expressed himself very pleased with the turn out stated the clothing was the best he had seen.	
	15/5/19		do	
	16/5/19		do	
	17/5/19		Released 10 "NR" at No 2 Ordnance Depot Blanc-fossés as usual	
	18/5/19		do	
	19/5/19		Relieved 4 P.O. at No Ordnance Depot Isowel	
	20/5/19		do	
	21/5/19		A tag on the verge. Road to very good	
	22/5/19		do	
	23/5/19		Road reconnaissance by available officers	
	24/5/19		Check parades for all denominations.	
	25/5/19		27 Duty Men demobilised	
	26/5/19		25 Duty Men demobilised	W

WAR DIARY
or
INTELLIGENCE SUMMARY.
(Erase heading not required.)

Army Form C. 2118.

Instructions regarding War Diaries and Intelligence Summaries are contained in F. S. Regs., Part II. and the Staff Manual respectively. Title pages will be prepared in manuscript.

Place	Date	Hour	Summary of Events and Information	Remarks and references to Appendices
Calais	27/8/19		Duties as usual	
	28/8/19		do	
	29/8/19		do 7 P.A.D. taken over, 1 Officer & 6 O.R. of total taken till 11.00 hours	
	30/8/19		do	
	31/8/19		do Shared Parade of all Denominations. Catalao stone	
			A D Hart Major	
			Commanding 5/6th Battalion Scottish Rifles	
			Strength of Battalion	
			Officers Other Ranks	
			25 409	
			Officers joined during month	
			Nil	
			Officers left during month	
			Lieut Blair M. to War Office	
			A D Hart Major	
			Commanding 5/6th Battalion Scottish Rifles	

Sheet 1.

5/6 S. Rifles

Army Form C. 2118.

WAR DIARY
INTELLIGENCE SUMMARY.
(Erase heading not required.)

60.O.
5 sheets

Place	Date	Hour	Summary of Events and Information	Remarks and references to Appendices
Calais	Monday 1st September		Battalion relieved from Vehicle Park Guard and 125 P of W Escort. Companies trained under Company arrangement.	
	Tuesday 2 Sept.		Relieved from Hand Gr. P of W Escort. Companies trained under Coy. arrangements.	
	Wednesday 3 Sept.		Three practices fired on the CALAIS RANGE by the Training Company. Musketing of General Class under R.S.M. All remaining available men on Musketing of General Class under R.S.M.	
	Thursday 4 Sept.		Training Company on the Range. General Class under Adjutant & R.S.M.	
	Friday 5 Sept.		The Battalion outfitted duties as usual, and training was carried out as follows:- All suitable men of B.L.A. Coys. paraded for instruction in Guard drill under the R.S.M. & the Signalling Class under the Signalling Officer. Lecture by the Adjutant on Discipline in the afternoon.	
	Saturday 6 Sept.		General Class under the Adjutant and R.S.M. Guards and duties as usual.	
	Sunday 7 Sept.		The Battalion attended the Presbyterian Church Parade in the Scottish Churches Hut, BEAUMARAIS. A team representing the Battalion proceeded to LILLE and played a football match against a team of FRENCH Civilians beating them by 2 goals to 1.	

Sheet 1.

WAR DIARY
or
INTELLIGENCE SUMMARY

Army Form C. 2118.

Place	Date	Hour	Summary of Events and Information	Remarks and references to Appendices
Calais	MONDAY 6 Sept.		The amalgamation of the 5th & 10th Battalions Scottish Rifles commenced. Letter "A" and "C" Companies under Major A.D. Hart proceeded to FORTINETTE'S and relieved the guards of the 10th Battalion there.	
	TUESDAY 9 Sept.		Amalgamation of the two Battalions concluded. HQrs. and Band D companies accepted both ETON and HARROW CAMPS. — No 6 Ordnance Depot Guard and all garrison duties found as usual.	
	WEDNESDAY 10th Sept.		Garrison Duties as usual. General Course made the Adjutant and R.S.M.	
	THURSDAY 11th Sept.		Garrison Duties as usual. Muster Parade held of all ranks in the afternoon and amalgamation Rolls Checked.	
	FRIDAY 12th Sept. SATURDAY 13 Sept.		Garrison Duties as usual.	
	SUNDAY 14th Sept.		No Church Parade in consequence of inclement weather. Garrison duties as usual.	
	MONDAY 15th Sept.		Garrison Duties as usual. Training:- Signalling Class under Signalling officer. Lewis Gun Class started under Lewis Gun Officer. Company training under Company Commanders.	
	Tuesday 16 Sept.		Garrison duties as usual. No General Class held. Company training carried out as usual.	

Sheet **III**.
WAR DIARY
INTELLIGENCE SUMMARY.
(Erase heading not required.)

Army Form C. 2118.

Instructions regarding War Diaries and Intelligence Summaries are contained in F.S. Regs., Part II. and the Staff Manual respectively. Title pages will be prepared in manuscript.

Place	Date	Hour	Summary of Events and Information	Remarks and references to Appendices
Calais	WEDNESDAY 17th Sept.		Garrison duties as usual. No general class held. Company training carried out as usual. Signalling class under "Signalling Officer".	
	THURSDAY 18th Sept.		Garrison Duties as usual. No general class held.	
	FRIDAY 19th Sept.		Demobilization of the remainder of the "Derby" and voluntarily enlisted men started. 40 men despatched to Dispersal Camps. Guards, garrison duties as usual.	
	SATURDAY 20th Sept.		60 Derby men despatched for demobilization. Guards duties as usual.	
	SUNDAY 21st Sept.		Battalion attended the Presbyterian Church Parade in the Scottish Churches Hut, Beaumarais.	
	MONDAY 22nd Sept.		25 "Derby" men proceeded home for demobilization. Guards and duties as usual.	
	TUESDAY 23rd Sept.		105 Derby men proceeded home for demobilization. Guards and garrison duties as usual.	
	WEDNESDAY 24th Sept.		60 Derby men proceeded home for demobilization. Guards and garrison duties as usual.	
	THURSDAY 25th Sept.		100 Derby men proceeded home for demobilization. Guards and garrison duties as usual.	

Sheet IV.
WAR DIARY
INTELLIGENCE SUMMARY.

(Erase heading not required.)

Army Form C. 2118.

Instructions regarding War Diaries and Intelligence Summaries are contained in F. S. Regs., Part II. and the Staff Manual respectively. Title pages will be prepared in manuscript.

Place	Date	Hour	Summary of Events and Information	Remarks and references to Appendices
Calais	FRIDAY 26/9/19		26 Derby men proceeded home for Demobilization. Guards and Garrison duties as usual.	
	SATURDAY 27/9/19		Guards and duties as usual. No more men proceeding home for Demobilization owing to the Railway Strike at home. All leave to the United Kingdom suspended, also for the same reason.	
	SUNDAY 28 Sept.		No church parade held owing to bad weather. The C.O. inspected the camp at 1200hrs.	
	MONDAY 29th Sept. TUESDAY 30th Sept.		Companies trained under Company arrangements. Guards and garrison duties as usual.	
			Strength as at. 30/9/19. Officers. 3& Other Ranks. 654.	
			Decorations. 43964 Sgt Smith L. awarded Belgian Croix de Guerre. Suppt to London Gazette, 11224 dated. 2/9/19.	

Sheet 1.

WARDIARY
INTELLIGENCE SUMMARY.
(Erase heading not required.)

Army Form C. 2118.

Place	Date	Hour	Summary of Events and Information	Remarks and references to Appendices
			Officers.	
			Joined during the month.	
			from 10th Scot Rifles. 8/9/19	
			Captain Macfaryd Seaforths	
			Lieut. Rock D. 2/ Lowland Garr.	
			" Wilson T. 4/ K.O.S.B	
			" Jack W.M.C. 6/ Scot Rifles	
			" Hope J. 3/ H.L.I.	
			" Paterson J.O. 5/ K.O.S.B.	
			" Scott W. 3/ K.O.S.B.	
			" Stuart R. 3/ Scot Rifles	
			" Wallace J. 5/ "	
			" Lahunie J. 6/ "	
			" McKenzie B. 5/ Sea. Highrs.	
			2/Lieut. Swann J.O. 5/H.L.I	
			" McKain E.J. 1/ Gordon H.N.	
			" Dawson W.E. 5/ Scot Rifles	
			" Ross W.L. 1/ H.L.I.	
			" Charleton J.R. 3/ K.O.S.B.	
			" Dick A.K. " "	
			Left Bath during the month.	
			2/Lieut. Smith + H.L.I. for discharge. 6.9.19	
			" Hall D.R. 9 Seaforths " " 22.9.19
			" Hawthorne 2/3 " " 22.9.19
			" Rose J.F. 1 Gunwood	22.9.19
			" Hamilton J. 9 Seaforths " "	22.9.19
			" Allen J.L. 3/H.L.I. " "	22.9.19
			" Hart W.A. 3 Seaforths " "	22.9.19
			" Montgomery W.M. 9 Seaforths for discharge	25.9.19

Signed,
Lieut Colonel
Commanding 5/6th Batt. Scottish Rifles

5/6 S.R.

Army Form C. 2118.

WAR DIARY
or
INTELLIGENCE SUMMARY.
(Erase heading not required.)

61. O.
6 sheet

Place	Date	Hour	Summary of Events and Information	Remarks and references to Appendices
Beaumarais Calais	1919 Oct 1st		Guards on the Yorkinetts Dumps and No. 6 Ordnance Repair Shops found as usual. Routine in camp. Attend to Hirlies routine.	
	2nd		Guards as usual. The whole Battalion was medically inspected at 14.00 hrs.	
	3rd		Guards as usual. The Battalion Transport moved up from York-Newlay to Canterbury Camp Beaumarais.	
	4th		Guards as usual.	
	5th		Guards found as usual. The Battalion attended Presbyterian Church parade at the Scottish Churches Hut Beaumarais at 10.30 hours. The Commanding Officer inspected the Camp and visited dinners.	
	6th		Guards found as usual. Letter 'B' Company found the General and fixing party at 14.30 hours for a corporal of the R.E.'s who died at No. 30 General Hospital, Calais. The Commanding Officer inspected Letter 'D' Company and all the Regimental Employly in Marrow Camp at 14.00 hours in full marching order.	

Instructions regarding War Diaries and Intelligence Summaries are contained in F. S. Regs., Part II. and the Staff Manual respectively. Title pages will be prepared in manuscript.

Army Form C. 2118.

WAR DIARY
or
INTELLIGENCE SUMMARY.
(Erase heading not required.)

Instructions regarding War Diaries and Intelligence Summaries are contained in F. S. Regs., Part II. and the Staff Manual respectively. Title pages will be prepared in manuscript.

Place	Date	Hour	Summary of Events and Information	Remarks and references to Appendices
Beaumarais Cuidia	1919 Oct 7		Petrol dumps etc Guards at Yorkietts and N°6 Ordnance Repair Shops Beaumarais found as usual. Guard for N°30 General Hospital also found by the Battalion.	
	8th		Guards found as yesterday. In the afternoon a Football match was played against the 6th Queens resulting in a draw of one goal each.	
	9th		Guards found as usual. Letter 'B' Company paraded in full marching order at 14.40 Hours for inspection by the commanding officer.	
	10th, 11th		Guards as usual.	
	12th		Guards as usual. Church parade in Scottish Church Nut at 10.30 Hours. The Battalion attended the Presbyterian Church parade in Scottish Church Nut at 10.30 Hours. The Commanding Officer inspected the Camp and billets at 12 Hours	
	13th		Guards as usual.	
	14th		Guards as usual. At 14.45 Hours a Football Match was played at the R.O.D. Football Ground at Yorkietts between teams	

Army Form C. 2118.

WAR DIARY
or
INTELLIGENCE SUMMARY.
(Erase heading not required.)

Instructions regarding War Diaries and Intelligence Summaries are contained in F. S. Regs., Part II. and the Staff Manual respectively. Title pages will be prepared in manuscript.

Place	Date	Hour	Summary of Events and Information	Remarks and references to Appendices
Beaumarais Calais	14th	Cont	representing B and D Companies (Beaumarais) and A and C Companies at (Fontinettes). After a very good game B and D Companies team won by 2 Goals to 1.	
	15th		Guards as usual.	
	16th		Guards as usual. 52 Derby and Voluntary enlisted men left for demobilization.	
	17th		Guards as usual.	
	18th		Guards as usual.	
	19th		Guards as usual. The Battalion attended the Presbyterian Church Parade at the Scottish Churches Hut at Beaumarais at 10.30 Hours. The Commanding Officer inspected the horses and harness at the Transport Section at 11.30 Hours.	
	20th		The Guard found by the Battalion at No 6 Ordnance Workshops was relieved by the 6th Queens. Other Guards as usual.	
	21st		Guards found as usual.	

Army Form C. 2118.

WAR DIARY
or
INTELLIGENCE SUMMARY.
(Erase heading not required.)

Place	Date	Hour	Summary of Events and Information	Remarks and references to Appendices
Beaumarais Calais	1919 Nov. 22nd		Guards found as usual. The Soldiers Christian Association Hut was opened in Eton Camp at 14.00 Hours. A Draft of 3 Officers and 172 Other ranks came from Gouville to be attached to the Battalion.	
"	23rd		Guards found as usual.	
	24th		Guards found as usual. The Battalion with the company of the 9th N.F.L attached paraded at 8.30 Hours. in full marching order and went for a Route March, the route being:- Beaumarais, Via Attacques, March and home via the Calais - Dunkerque Road arriving back in Camp at 13.15 Hours.	
	25th		In addition to the Guards already found by the Battalion the Guards found by the 6th Queens at No. 2 Ordnance Depot, No. 6 Ordnance Depot and the Vehicle Park were taken over by the Battalion.	
	26th		Guards found as usual. The Battalion attended the Presbyterian Church Parade at Scottish Churches Nat. Beaumarais at 10.30 Hours.	

Army Form C. 2118.

WAR DIARY
or
INTELLIGENCE SUMMARY.
(Erase heading not required.)

Place	Date	Hour	Summary of Events and Information	Remarks and references to Appendices
Beaumarais Calais.	1919 27th		Guards found as usual.	
	28.		The Guards found at Montinette were taken over by the 17th Royal Fusiliers, and the half Battalion on detachment at Yoslinette left their camp there during the afternoon and marched up and rejoined Head Quarters. Orders were received for the Battalion to be moved to Calais at once and the immediate demobilization of the rest of the Battalion. The Guards in the Beaumarais Area were found as usual.	
	29.		The Guards in the Beaumarais Area were found as usual. by the Battalion. Later A Company proceeded to No 6 N.Z. Camp for demobilization.	
	30.		Guards found as usual. 60 men proceeded for demobilization	
	31.		With the exception of No 30. General Hospital Guard still found by the Battalion, the whole of the other Guards were taken over by the Hampshire Regiment. 66 men proceeded for demobilization	

WAR DIARY
or
INTELLIGENCE SUMMARY.
(Erase heading not required.)

Army Form C. 2118.

Place	Date	Hour	Summary of Events and Information	Remarks and references to Appendices
			Strength of Unit. 2nd November 1919. 29 Officers 262 Other Ranks.	
			[signature] Lieut Colonel Commanding 5th Scottish Rifles.	

www.ingramcontent.com/pod-product-compliance
Lightning Source LLC
Chambersburg PA
CBHW081552160426
43191CB00011B/1910